Unruly

UNRULY

THE HIGHS AND LOWS OF BECOMING A MAN

Ja Rule

WITH KIM GREEN

A FLAVOR UNIT BOOK

Amistad

An Imprint of HarperCollins*Publishers*

HarperCollins books may be purchased for educational, business, or sales promotional use. For information, please e-mail the Special Markets Department at SPsales@harpercollins.com.

FIRST EDITION

Library of Congress Cataloging-in-Publication Data has been applied for.

ISBN: 978-0-06-231617-2

14 15 16 17 18   OV/RRD   10 9 8 7 6 5 4 3 2 1

This book is dedicated to my foundation—my family, who is responsible for my growth: my grandparents Edward Cherry and Mary Cherry; my parents, William Jeffrey Atkins (rest in peace) and Debra Atkins; my wife, Aisha; and my children, Brittney, Jordan and Jeff Jr.

CONTENTS

Part I
Venni Vetti Vecci

Part II
The Last Temptation

Part III
Pain Is Love

I do not speak about my exploits with pride. I'm not trying to glorify or glamorize what it took to get me to this point. My only hope is that these memories of my life may save you some pain. Give love.

PART ONE

Venni Vetti Vecci

PROLOGUE

———

THE CORRECTIONS OFFICERS WERE ALL BITCHES. THEY SPOKE to us like the animals that they had made us. There was no respect for any of us, not even me, who had sold 30 million records, traveled the world, won countless awards and flown to meetings on private jets. Who would think a bitch-ass corrections officer would be the one to show *me* something that I should have already known?

Oneida Correctional Facility in Rome, New York, had a reputation among inmates for being a prison with racist COs and rampant misconduct among its officers. The officers would patrol the yard, always listening for some bit of conversation to get a sense of what the inmates were thinking.

It was another uneventful day in the prison yard as the sun shone on the rusty chain link fences highlighting the age and neglect of the facility. The yard always held a crisp feeling of weighty expectancy, always waiting anxiously for something to jump off. In some corners of the yard, there were the bulky inmates lifting weights, while others concentrated on their chess games. Others just stared into space, dreaming of the day when their prison nightmare would end.

Officer Smith, one of the more difficult officers, was nicknamed "the Klansman." The Klansman may have been my age or a little younger. He had evil dark blue eyes and slicked-back hair, which revealed his large forehead. His beer belly was bursting through his tight uniform shirt.

"You know, Atkins, your kids are job security for my kids," Officer Smith said. He just looked at me as if he had said something innocent but what he was really saying was that the cycle never gets broken for Black people.

I could feel my rage bubbling up in my stomach. The urge to choke the shit out of him was overwhelming. The only reason I didn't was because I knew that fights in the yard only caused sirens to flash, twenty-four-hour lockdowns and a lot of unnecessary paperwork.

The only thing I could safely say in response was, "Not *my* kids."

Smith didn't know what to say to that. He had assumed a whole lot about me based on the color of my skin. He wasn't expecting me to say shit back at all. That muthafucka didn't even *know* me, my family or what we've been through. I may have been in prison, but it was partly because muthafuckas with an agenda put me there and partly because of my own doing.

"I'm not supposed to be here," I whispered under my breath.

Officer Smith was already gone. He walked away not knowing the weight of his words. My head was heavy trying to hold them.

I wasn't *supposed* to be here, in prison, but I was. I knew then that it was my fault and my fault only. There were no more excuses. This was just one of those fucked-up Black-people moments, where we learn truths about ourselves through our oppressor's eyes. It was enlightening to understand how white people see us, as fucking *job security*. In his mind, Officer Smith, his sons and his grandsons will further their family's mission of holding Black men down in prison. They will be the keepers of "our place." It's scary to admit, but in some ways, it's kinda true.

We don't have to be someone's fucking legacy, keeping them employed by our irresponsibility and disrespect for our communities and ourselves. Our lives mean so much more than that. Our ancestors went through too much for us to be free for me and other Black people to be doing stupid shit that gets us locked up.

After the conversation with CO Smith, I told my homies what that bitch CO had said to me. "See, he didn't say it to y'all, he said it to *me*, the most successful muthafucka in here. He was trying to break our spirits, man. He must not have understood that we are descendants of a strong race of people. We come from the Black Panthers, Martin Luther King Jr., Malcolm X, Rosa Parks. How dare that muthafucka belittle me? We can't let them break us. We can't."

Eyes widened. Everyone was blindsided by the deep blow that had just been thrown. Several of them put their heads down, ashamed to even look at each other.

That's just what they expect from us. What they don't expect is for us to get the fuck outta here . . .

ONE

———

Silence

I WAS ONLY FOUR YEARS OLD WHEN MY FATHER CAME IN THE
house yelling about some dumb shit. "You should be learning,
boy! Not playing with all those toys."

My Moms could smell my father's anger mounting again.
She could sniff out that rancid scent that she had become too
familiar with. The stench of his anger seeped from his every
pore. This was an aroma that made her fear for my life and
her own.

My father's tone was particularly harsh that day, and as
he railed at me for holding a toy, my Moms recognized that
glassy look in his eyes. She could tell that her husband had
been somewhere that he didn't belong. Moms never wanted
me to be on the receiving side of my father's blows. She had
taken enough of them herself. There had been too many silent

nights of her nursing her wounds with drugstore ice packs and old towels.

That night was not unlike all the rest. He was always yelling about something. My Moms came over to me, scooped me up off the wood floor and placed me in my room. She was proud that we had two bedrooms. The second bedroom would come in handy the night she would change our lives forever.

She trembled as she thought, *"At least, I have Jeffrey. He's worth everything I'm about to do."* In my room, behind a closed door, I played with the toy that she'd given me. While I lost myself in it, I was losing my Dad, at the same time.

MOMS WALKED BACK into the living room and said to her husband, "Nigga, this is the night you gon' die. I've been stupid enough to take these beatings, but if you're going to abuse my son, like you've been abusing me, that's not going down."

My father never said a word to her. He didn't argue. He didn't say, "I'll change," or "You know I would never hurt Little Jeff." Or even, "I love you."

"I understand," is all he said. And then there was silence.

Moms called my grandmother and said calmly into the phone, "I'm leaving Jeff today. I can't take it anymore."

My grandmother put her second husband on the phone. Grandpa Cherry okayed the arrangement. He said, "Yes, I'll come get you and Little Jeff."

And that was that. There was to be no more yelling and

cursing. There was to be no more hitting. And there was to be no more puffy eyes and salty tear stains for Moms to try to hide. There was just to be no more daddy.

That is how he left us. With silence.

MY MOTHER MET MY FATHER at a party in 1974. As soon as William Jeffrey Atkins walked in the door with his half-cut T-shirt and muscular body, she immediately noticed him. She says that he was "quite interesting." Moms admired his burgundy polyester bell-bottoms and how they hugged his slim frame. She watched her husband-to-be float into the room without a word. It wasn't until the end of the evening that he finally approached her.

"Didn't you notice me looking at you? I think I've met you before," he said.

They danced briefly to James Brown's "The Payback," which was the anthem of the streets at the time. The song exalted Black folks' new sense of freedom while acknowledging our collective rage. After they danced, he said, "I'm leaving now, but I'd like to call you. I'll get a pen and paper. I'll be back."

My mother worried that the handsome stranger would float into the crowd, never to return. When he did, my mother went to a nearby table so she could write. The syrupy sound of Tavares' "She's Gone" warmed the room. Couples danced and kissed under the colorful lights and the sparkles of the disco ball. It put her into a romantic mood. On the scrap of paper, she neatly wrote "Debra Ann Moorehand, 208 100th Avenue; Hollis, Queens, 11423," and "718-656-3234."

William said, smiling, "I didn't plan on writing you, I was just going to call you."

Her eagerness slightly embarrassed her. She whispered, "Just in case you wanted to write or come by . . . someday."

As they said their goodbyes, William Jeffrey Atkins promised to call.

He didn't call for days.

When he finally did, Debra suggested that William pick her up from school. William didn't realize that Debra Moorehand was still in high school. He was a few months younger than her. He had graduated from Food and Maritime Trade School and was an aspiring baker. He agreed to pick her up after school, but with a warning: "I'll have a tie on. I'm job hunting."

Shit went quick between them two. They dated heavily and fell in love, all within a year. Before Moms knew it, William Jeffrey Atkins was asking her to be his wife. When Moms graduated from Central Commercial High School at seventeen, she walked down the aisle not only with a boyfriend but also with a tiny diamond engagement ring on her finger. They married on September 14, 1974, when she was eighteen.

"I always felt safe with your father. No one was going to bother me with him around," Moms later told me. Although my mother was comfortable that my Dad was making $500 a week, once he started working, she didn't realize that he was also picking up a bunch of new friends with some very bad habits.

TWO YEARS LATER, a leap year, I was born on the rare twenty-ninth day of the shortest month of the year. That would be my first and last birthday celebration. We were Jehovah's Witnesses, so birthdays were not celebrated. The only thing my family ever did was cook a special birthday dinner after the fact. No one even said "happy birthday" to me. They didn't believe in it.

Moms worked as a secretary at Creedmoor Psychiatric Center right up until the week I was born. Every morning she would take me to my grandmother's house, work at Creedmoor from eight to four, pick me up at four thirty, take me home, make dinner and clean the house while my father was hanging out in the Village with his new friends and their bad habits.

Soon, Moms and me started to linger at my grandmother's house every evening, allowing Moms a little time to catch up with my grandmother and hear about the things that I had done to make her laugh that day. I was a well-behaved child and my father's sisters used to argue with each other over who would take care of me. We would all comfortably sink into the darkening folds of night, passing time and catching up. My grandmother and mother would reminisce about me being in the school play. I was playing Scrooge in *A Christmas Carol.* There were two of us originally given the role because the play was really long. On the day of our performance the other kid was sick. My teacher had asked me to do that kid's part, as well as my own. The teacher quickly decided that I would have to write down the other kid's lines on the inside of the robe. I did the roles so well that the audience gave me a standing ovation.

My grandmother was proud. Moms giggled with pride. I loved when my grandmother told that story. It gave me a hint that I was made to entertain. That was the first time I felt the rush of being onstage.

Another evening after we got back to our pristine two bedroom apartment on the third floor of a walk-up in Queens Village, Moms cleaned the already clean house, made dinner for the two of us, gave me a bath and laid out my clothes for the next day. Tired, but not ready to go to sleep, she sat on the couch to read a book, while I played on the floor at her feet.

The young baker busted in and lashed out at Moms. In a rage, he grabbed the book out of her hands and started ripping out the pages, one by one, and then tore them into tiny pieces. He then threw them into the air, sending confetti-like scraps into the air that showered down on my head like snow.

It was on.

My mother was ready to fight. My father punched her in the eye with such force that her brown eye turned black as night. After the scuffle, when she looked in the mirror, she knew she couldn't go to work the next day. The days ticked by but there was no improvement in her eye. Reluctantly, she returned to work with a new accessory: shades.

Mom's supervisor, also a Black woman, with a folksy, down-to-earth style, was surprised by the new look. She teased her, saying, "*Girl*, you need to take those sunglasses off. You must have gotten your ass beat last night." My mother was so shocked and humiliated that all she could do was slowly remove the glasses that were meant to hide the truth of her marriage. The supervisor was speechless.

The ugliness of my mother's ravaged eye sobered her supervisor. She looked into my mother's troubled eyes and said, "Debra, it will happen again. You can't stay. You must leave now or it will go on. There are places you can go. There are shelters."

My mother didn't listen.

Another time, my parents were at a wedding and my father slipped away to wander around the banquet hall to see what other party he could crash. When Moms realized that he was gone, she went to find him. Moms bragged, "It was my turn to act crazy."

She found my father dancing and flirting with another woman. My father was always womanizing. It's almost like he did it just to make Moms mad. The humiliation, anger and shame must have choked her. She grabbed an umbrella from the hall, stormed out of the building and went to the parking lot. She walked over to their car and attempted to bust the windshield. My Dad followed her and watched her unsuccessfully assaulting the car. He came up behind her and they started going at it in the parking lot, until my uncle stopped them. When my uncle finally got them in the car, he drove and they fought all the way home, my father throwing sloppy punches over the leather seats. My Moms always said, "No one could stop him when he was enraged."

Moms could see that my father's new habits were starting to have a grip on him. She pretended that things were going well but she knew that they weren't. Although my father was still making good money, he was also squandering it away to buy more drugs.

Moms knew in her heart that her marriage was already over. When she learned that she was pregnant, again, she was devastated. She gathered the strength to confess her fears to my father. "I'm thinking of not going through with this pregnancy."

In response he said, "Whatever you want to do will be fine for me." Moms scheduled an abortion and her girlfriend, Diane, agreed to go with her.

Diane talked Moms' ear off all day before the appointment. "Debbie, I'll take care of the baby, if you don't want it," she finally said.

"I'm not going to carry a baby for nine whole months and then give it to someone else. That's just not right," Moms said.

Moms just braced herself for being a single mother of two. After all, her own mother had struggled with four. Moms remembered her own childhood with a lonely mother whose drunken first husband, Moms' father, was living in the bottle. My Moms and her siblings were all latchkey kids. Moms knew she *could* survive, even if it meant that my little sister and me would let ourselves into an empty apartment, with only the streets to raise us.

MOMS CARRIED THE BABY from March to November. It was the autumn of my fifth year and the pregnancy was almost over. Although she was going to the doctor for her regular checkups, the hospitals weren't using high-tech ultrasound machines to check on babies in the hood. That shit was for rich people, I guess. Back then, as long as the doctor heard a heartbeat they told the mother that she and the baby were fine.

During the last month of the pregnancy, my Aunt Kathy asked Moms an innocent question, as they sat in the Atkins kitchen, shooting the shit. "Debra, has the baby been kicking?"

My Moms knew at that moment that something might be wrong. No one had asked that question during the whole nine months. Moms thought back to her first pregnancy and the hell I put her through with my constant kicking and moving. I had been eager for life.

"This baby girl is just lazy, not like my Jeffrey," Moms told herself and Aunt Kathy. The very next day when she went to the doctor, he said he couldn't hear the heartbeat anymore.

Only silence.

The doctor said that the baby was just floating inside of Moms, not even fully developed, even though Moms had been getting fatter over the past nine months. My father had been using cocaine and selling it for over a year. That might have had something to do with how the pregnancy got fucked-up.

The doctor sent Moms home with a dead baby in her belly, saying that she should deliver the baby "naturally." Later that same day, Moms was overcome with pain. When the baby finally did come out, the delivery was effortless. Moms didn't even have to push. The nurse took the baby away. Moms refused to look at the twisted sight of an almost-life.

"I turned her into a person by giving her a name: *Kristen*," Moms said, longingly.

The only solid explanation that my five-year-old mind was offered was Moms' terse words: "Kristen was stillborn." I didn't understand, really, but I sensed the ache of emptiness that was familiar.

As a child I didn't understand death. I wasn't there to grieve with my mother after my sister was stillborn. It wasn't until later on in my life that I grieved. I talk about Kristen's death in my song "Daddy's Little Baby," as well as my daughter Brittany's birth. I always wanted a sibling. But it never happened. I carry Kristen in my heart. She's a constant reminder that responsibility comes with being alive.

This means early on I was a survivor.

*

July 11, 2011

Today I can truly say I've been through it all. A young kid comes in today and they put him in the 18 cell right next to mine. He looked kinda depressed coming in but nothing out of the ordinary. A few hours go past and all of a sudden I hear someone choking. He's trying to kill his self. We all heard it. Everyone runs to their cell doors and start kicking, banging and calling the COs. Now, I've seen a person get shot and I've even seen someone die from a drug overdose, but this was different, this was suicide. It was like I could hear the life leaving his body. The COs rush in the cell and save him. I didn't even think some shit like this was possible in these cells. He tied his bed sheet to a pole that's attached to a sink, which is about 3 feet off the ground. He made some sort of noose, wrapped it around his neck and then threw himself forward into a boston crab carmel clutch type position. I never understood why a person would wanna kill themselves. Life is love & love is living. It's God's most precious gift. After they brought him back to his cell in the suicide suit, he cried for hours. We tried to console him, telling him it's never that bad to wanna kill yourself. Turns out he just turned 18 and got a girlfriend who is only 16. Her parents pressed charges and now he's locked up on sex offender charges. He was in school for graphic arts to learn how to make video games. It's sad 'cause he's still a kid, himself—a good kid, at that. Now, he'll be forever labeled rapist or sex offender when really he's probably just a kid in love. Wow it's crazy how 2 years can be so close but yet so far when you're 18 & 16. It seems far because he's now an adult and she's still a teen. When you're 10 & 12 it's cute and innocent. When you're 18 & 20 nobody gives a fuck.

It makes me think about Britt and her starting to date. I'm not gonna lie, at 18 & 16 I'd be at a crossroad, too, but to ruin a young man's life & stain his future is not right. At 18 you're legally an adult but you're really still just a kid. I remember when I was 18, I thought I knew everything about life & living, as I look back now, as a 35 year old man, I realize I didn't know shit. LOL I'm still learning & growing as a man. 2 years, that's what separates me from my family right now. I look at it as short time but yet when Ish told me that Britt's acting partner was 17 I almost had a fit, even tho she'll be 16 soon and I'm sure he'll be 18 soon, and BAM, there it is, a crossroad. LOL. It's funny how God puts situations in front of you so you can see it clearly. I trust Britt. I know me & Ish raised her well. Besides she hates Kids. LOL. But I also know the intentions of a young man. I got my eyes on you, lil homie. Don't make me come back to this motherfucker!

*

TWO

—

Moaning

THERE WAS A LOT OF CONFUSION AFTER MY FATHER LEFT. I was six years old when he moved to Florida. Things were tough for Moms, the bills and the pressure were crushing her. Although my parents were still in contact, my father wasn't paying a dime of child support. Moms never bothered to take him to court, which showed her pride and strength. With only one child, she figured that she would just struggle like everyone else—never welfare, never food stamps.

Our neighborhood was filled with Black single mothers with too many kids and not enough money to feed them all. The streets were lined with men who had abandoned their children for the street. But, there were many middle-class, two-parent families sprinkled throughout the neighborhood. There were also co-ops nearby where people lived decently.

Even though folks were struggling to make ends meet, there was a strong sense of community. There was hope.

Later, though, when I was nine or ten, that's when drugs hit the neighborhood hard. That's when the streets began to feel worn. Every day, busy mothers and their children passed back and forth through the streets, constantly praying not to be the next random victim of a stray bullet or a desperate soul. Clouds seemed to hang over the whole neighborhood, even when the sun was shining.

It was my grandparents' virtue and love that led them to help Moms, who was struggling emotionally and financially. They suggested that I come and live with them for a while.

"We can provide a more stable home for Little Jeff," Grandpa Cherry said.

WHEN I WAS SIX YEARS OLD, every Tuesday night was spent in the basement of 208-08 100th Avenue, Queens, New York 11429. The house was a modest two-story, three-bedroom yellow brick house on a side street, which was part of a small deceptive enclave of "suburban" homes.

Every day, when I came home from school, my grandmother's house hugged me with the aroma of fried chicken and collard greens. My grandmother would help me with my homework while feeding me forkfuls of joy. The house was full of life. My grandmother had two more children with Cherry, my Uncle Dennis and my Aunt Dawn. They were five and seven years older than me, which made me feel like I was part of a big family.

My grandfather Ed Cherry, "Papa," spent most of his days in that house sleeping. Cherry was a big, strict man with medium-brown skin and large hands. He wore a military buzz cut and had a distinctive gap between his two front teeth. He wanted things a certain way, *his* way. And whenever things weren't like he wanted, Cherry clenched his jaw and then opened his mouth as wide as he could and yelled. Whenever he was mad, all I remembered was that gap in his teeth. It was the siren before the storm.

My grandfather worked at night at the post office and later for the New York City Transit Authority. He always held two or three jobs at one time. Grandpa Cherry hustled jobs, not money. He did plumbing, welding and was a cabbie. He showed me that I got my hustling skills naturally.

When I was growing up in the house, anyone who woke Cherry up during the day was getting an ass whooping. There is no polite way to describe what happened when Cherry was mad. He was a dragon coming out of a cave. When he came out of that room, somebody's ass was getting lit on fire, because he was breathing it. It was as simple as that. It was usually me and Dennis getting beat. My Aunt Dawn was always spared.

Living under "Papa's" roof provided me with my first example of a responsible man. There was always plenty of everything that we needed in the house—especially the fear that only fathers can bring. Unlike the other men that I grew up around, my grandfather was the only man who had a wife and family whom he cared for. My grandmother never worked and Cherry never minded working several jobs to take care of the household so that my grandmother could take care of us.

As I grew up, I remembered Cherry and his insistence that we stay on the straight and narrow, and follow Jehovah, always. Although Cherry's strict discipline didn't work on me and Dennis during those days, living under his roof helped me at least understand what men are supposed to be.

What I *never* understood was why we had to have Bible study on Tuesday nights. It was a rehashing of the actual Public Meeting that had just taken place on Sunday at Kingdom Hall. The Jehovah's Witnesses typically met three or more times a week. After meeting at the Kingdom Hall, another night they met for *Watchtower* study so that they could discuss articles from the *Watchtower* magazine, and the third meeting of the week was held at an elder's home. Each member was considered an ordained minister and eligible to run meetings.

I can still recall my heart sinking on Tuesday nights whenever the doorbell chimed. I would run upstairs and peek out of the window at the hungry Jehovah Witnesses standing on the other side of our door, ready for the good news that my grandfather, the elder, would deliver straight from the mouth of Jehovah.

When we weren't in the basement enduring those endless rants of self-righteousness and morality, we were out on the streets hand-delivering Jehovah's message door-to-door like pizzas. Instead of pizza, we offered pamphlets and magazines called *Awake!* and *Watchtower.* Papa told me that the magazines were intended to "build confidence in the secure new world to replace the wicked, lawless system of things."

We were always dressed neatly when we did field service. My grandfather wore his dark blue raincoat and shiny black military shoes. Even me, I was in my dress pants and my white starched-collared shirt. Grandma always made me wear my church shoes, even though they hurt my feet. When we rang the doorbells, most people reacted as though they hadn't ordered what we were bringing. The people were polite enough, but I could tell that they were eager for us to leave. The Jehovah's belief system clearly didn't fit with the raggedy landscape that surrounded us, merely three blocks away on the Boulevard, where the code of the street was simple: "get money." What we were bringing wasn't what the people needed. Only the Witnesses thought it was worthy of their pushy persistence.

Three blocks over was the ghetto in all of its pain and splendor. It was the hood, where Black men were willing to risk everything for dollar bills. The area consisted of corner bodegas, walk-up tenements and the infamous high rises, affectionately known as "the projects."

For the next six years, this wildlife reserve filled with horrid smells and loud voices was to be my new home. It was the wholesome environment that my grandparents had promised. The visions of heaven that the Jehovah's were jabbering about at people's front doors seemed too far removed from the eighties' crack epidemic that was redefining desperation.

I just hated the thought of "field service," which we had to do every week. Right before Cherry said, "Let's get ready to go," I would grab my stomach, scrunch up my face and plead the pain of stomach cramps. If that didn't work, I would grab my throat and pretend that I had come down with laryngitis. Grandpa Cherry, the Dragon, never wavered. "Ain't nothing wrong with you, boy! Do you want me to get my belt?"

Grandpa Cherry would whip my ass with anything he could get his hands on, including belts and electrical cords.

As we walked through the neighborhood, I was in charge of holding the magazines. I could hear the distant sounds of hip-hop flooding out of every car. Although my exposure to the world was supposed to be limited, I was well aware of the songs that every boy had on the tip of their tongue. These rhymes were the first time that I heard the voices of young Black men. "My Adidas" by Run DMC was the anthem of the street. Later, I would actually get to see DMC riding through the neighborhood in his 850i BMW. He had his gold dope dookie rope chain with the Adidas hanging from it.

Papa never smiled, he always just scowled and shook his head, hating the loud booming beats of disrespect. The music seemed to get louder and louder every day. The music was drowning out the sounds of sirens that defined our lives. Cherry didn't care for the music. I was familiar with those songs and obviously feeling them. I was forced to ignore them, as impossible as that was.

Cherry said that I was forbidden to play with kids that weren't Jehovah's Witnesses because those were the rules of the religion. That was cool because most of them also believed as I did: *Jehovah was not for me.* There were other kids in the neighborhood like Chris Black, Otha and my man E-Funk that I ended up being mad close to. I hung with the kids who were Jehovah's Witnesses and who were just as bad as the others.

The "rebellers" and me all hung together while the elders got one step closer to heaven, which was a far climb from our basement. Rich Nealy was good friends with my Uncle Dennis and since they were older than us they tried hard to be like John and Dave, who were older than them and already in trouble. Me, Jonathan and Brent were the young guys, trying to be like Trevor, Dennis and Rich. We were all closer than homies so we called each other "cousins." When me, Brent and Jonathan rode our bikes, the ride was always bumpy as we navigated the little red-and-green covered caps that littered the streets. We rode over them with the skill and grit of cowboys.

"Rich Nealy can't come over here anymore," Cherry announced one day. Something was missing from the house and Cherry swore that Rich had taken it. "That Nealy boy is no good." My grandfather knew that Dave, Rich's older brother, was selling drugs. I didn't know about all the trouble they were in, I just looked up to them and tried to get into it, too. Cherry knew everything they were doing because he's the one who disfellowshipped them all.

WHEN I WAS eight or nine, I was sent to spend the summer with my Uncle Bruce. At the time, he was one of the most successful people in my family. He was the first with some real money. He was an executive at Xerox or something. He lived in this huge house in Memphis. I knew immediately, when I saw his humongous house, that it was the life I wanted to live when I got older. Uncle Bruce had a house and a family. My cousin Smitty also had a nice house. His was in Long Island. I would go out there sometime and he'd take me to play racquetball.

Even though I was young, I recognized that every example of success in front of me was in a union of marriage and family. My immediate family, my Moms and me, were struggling. Grandpa Cherry had a structured family and he was able to make it. Early on, this taught me that I needed stability in my family first in order to have any amount of success. Even today, successful people only want to be around other family-oriented, successful people. It means that you are stable. No one wants a loose cannon around.

The union of marriage and the structure it provides is important in our society. It is sometimes frowned upon in the corporate setting when you don't have the stability of a family unit. The single guy is not looked upon favorably. I recognized these signs early on. I didn't want to be like my father. I was determined that I was going to be there for my kids.

WHILE I WAS LIVING with my grandparents, Moms moved from apartment to apartment. Most of the time she had a one bedroom, other times she had a studio apartment, depending on the rent. When the rent got too tough for her, she would move somewhere cheaper. Despite her instability, she always picked me up from my grandparents' house on the weekends or on her days off.

Moms was living on 195th Street. We called it 1-9-5. Like all of the other single mothers, she, too, shuffled down the boulevard, running to get to her low-paying job on time. From time to time Moms would announce, "I'm taking a test to get a promotion." My Moms had big dreams for us. Moms would take these state tests and she always passed them. The first time, she was promoted out of the office where she had been doing secretarial work, and then she was promoted onto the ward with the patients.

After Moms did that she took another test to become a ward supervisor with six therapists on her shift that she was responsible for. Moms even took the patients on trips to ballgames and the circus. These were all things she could have been doing with me, if things had been different. The eight-to-four shift that she originally had was okay, but Moms still wanted to do better. She decided to go back to school to study nursing. In order to do that, she needed to request the late shift so she could go to school during the day.

For six grueling months, she took nursing classes during the day and worked at night at the hospital. It was too much and soon she became overwhelmed. When she dropped out of nursing school, she asked for her day shift back, but it was no longer available. Four-to-twelve was the shift that she would have to keep.

My father tried to keep in touch. Every time he did, he just made a bigger mess of things. My father was in New York when I was about nine years old. He had called my grandparents to see if he could take me out for a slice of pizza. I was excited to see him, but sad that I didn't know him like I should have. After I spent an hour with him, I saw who he was, and in many ways, I am just like him.

At the pizza restaurant, my father got our slices and I took mine and went to the bar where you get garlic and crushed pepper. A man saw me and reached over me to get the garlic.

"What the hell are you doing? Don't ever reach over my son's food," my father said. He proceeded to beat the hell out of that man. He was showing me that men have to protect their family.

While Moms was going through all those changes with her job, I was going through some significant changes of my own. Contrary to Cherry's wishes, I did have some friends that were not Witnesses, because Moms had worldly friends and they had worldly sons. Tyray was one of those.

The first time I had sex, I was eleven years old and it was orchestrated by my "cousin" Tyray, who was thirteen years old. Tyray approached me one day, saying, "Yo. Jeff, do you want to do it?" I wasn't sure what he was referring to, but I figured it must be sex. I could tell from his hushed tone, which was usually reserved for conversations about chicks. He continued, "I got two nasty little girls from around the way and they agreed to do it with us."

"Okay." I figured if Tyray was doing it, it would be okay for me to do it, too.

Back then, we were break-dancing and we stored cardboard boxes in the stairwells of the Woodhull projects so that we would have a flat surface to break on when we were over there. Tyray had a different idea for the flattened cardboard.

Once we collected the boxes from behind the stairwell, the four of us took the elevator to the top floor in nervous silence. Then we found the staircase that led to the roof, which was never really used. When we all reached the landing, the pungent smell of urine was almost palpable. The flicker of the broken fluorescent lights dimmed the stairwell further, creating a broken-down-disco effect. The stairs were sticky with dried piss, Old English and grape soda. Tyray laid the cardboard down as if he was preparing a bed for queens. He laid the two pieces of cardboard right next to each other on the stair landing, like two twin beds.

There was no conversation, flirting or even introducing ourselves to the girls. They were both noticeably heavy with no makeup or anything. They were plain, but I figured it was the best I could do when I wasn't even looking for sex that day. *Tyray was a funny dude.* Me and Tyray banged those chicks right there. Side by side. It was quick, uncomfortable, and *wack.* It was more about getting it in quickly before someone caught us.

Once I was on top of my chick, I closed my eyes tightly, trying to feel the thing that the homies promised I'd feel. I only felt myself breathing hard like I did when I was shooting hoops, but it was supposed to be like the deep, guttural breathing that I'd seen in pornos. I'm sure the girl was hoping that it would be over soon, too. Tyray knew what he was doing, at least more than I did. It was over before I knew it. Both of the girls looked flustered and embarrassed. We watched them as they slowly went down the stairs to leave the building. We all smiled awkward smiles and waved goodbye.

After a little more practice, I realized that I loved this thing called sex. The chicks around the way wanted to do it as much as I did, so I did it with as many girls as I could. There were so many different girls and everyone was doing it in so many different ways. I had girls agree to do it in the park, up against trees, in elevators, bathrooms, you name it. I loved sex like I loved music. It was something strictly for the senses and it was risky. Sex is the universal escape, so it was always plentiful in the hood.

Moms was also aware of the great escape. She got disfellowshipped because she told on herself. She could have held on to the illusion of her faithfulness a little tighter, but she bravely decided to do what most Witnesses wished they could do, free themselves. She had been leading a double life for too long; going to the Kingdom Hall on Friday nights, even sometimes dragging me with her. Then, she would drop me back to my grandparents, and change clothes to meet her friends and boyfriend at the bar.

When she couldn't take it anymore, Moms called a meeting with the elders and laid it all out. "I'm not living in accordance with the laws and I'm tired of living a double life." She continued, "God sees everything I'm doing, anyway. The only people I'm fooling are you and the rest of the congregation."

Silence.

The elders, Cherry included, didn't know what to say. "Debbie, you are well liked in the congregation. We don't have to disfellowship you. We could just put you on *reprove*. You'll just need to turn away from your worldly ways." Being on reprove meant that she could still attend Kingdom Hall.

Moms boldly said to the elders, " I don't think I want to stop doing what I'm doing."

"We have no other choice than to let you go . . ." the elders responded.

Jehovah lost yet another Witness and Moms never returned to Kingdom Hall again. *Free at last.*

CHERRY AND MY GRANDMOTHER saw no other choice but to distance themselves from Moms, which meant me, too. Even her older brother, Bruce, completely cut her off. Moms often asked me with tears in her eyes, "How can they turn their back on me?"

I was proud of Moms, though. I wanted her to know that I wanted to be with her. If she was going to be the black sheep of the family, she wasn't going out like that alone. I had seen things and heard people talking about getting disfellowshipped. I understood the concept, but the practice still made no sense. To this day, Moms is totally turned off by religion. Now she just reads her Bible alone, praying that God can even hear her.

There we were, another Black family divided because of the most lethal drug of them all, *religion*. I know it broke my grandparents' hearts to turn their backs on Moms and me. I could feel that my grandparents knew in their hearts that they had to get away from Kingdom Hall and Hollis, Queens. My grandparents sold their house and moved to Virginia.

I was almost twelve. My grandparents had helped Moms for almost six years. It was time for me to go back to my Moms, where I belonged. My grandparents had taken me through elementary school while Moms got back on her feet. They had gotten me through the worst of it. Or so they thought.

I was heading back home as a young man with some questions churning in my head and heart. I had returned to the hood. The hopelessness hung heavily in the air. Drugs were all over the morning, afternoon and late-night news. The row of stores that we walked by everyday was indelibly printed on my brain. The stores that stayed open late lit the way for all of us to reach our destinations safely. Every day of my life, Moms and me walked past Guzman Foods, the Check Cashing place, Chinese Kitchen, Pizza, Wines and Liquors and the 99-Cent Store, which were the glue that held the hood together. The other side of the street was the dark side, where empty lots were weakly protected by dangling barbed wire fences that only served to create a place for mischievous young men to lurk.

Drugs were all over everyone's life like a sticky glue that we couldn't get off of us.

IN JUNIOR HIGH SCHOOL, my crew was Jason and Kavin. I was sort of the leader of our group because I had the craziest ideas and I was always planning some shit to do. People with ideas tend to be leaders. It was with them that my escapades with partying began. We actually started slowly and innocently. Our first joints were filled with oregano. We didn't get real weed until we started going to Jason's corner store in Laurel-ton called Pop and Kims, where the older guys hung out. It was a favorite spot in the hood because they stored the 40s in the ice cream freezer, so they were extra cold. One of the older guys offered us some real weed one time, and after that, we never took out the oregano again.

For us to be kids that young we had big personalities. My homies Devin and Jason both had light skin and Kavin was darker. I was somewhere in the middle and we all had fresh flattops or Gumby haircuts. We thought we were *the shit*.

SOMETIMES, WHEN MOMS came home after midnight, on the weekends, she would smell us smoking weed in the lobby of the building. Hiding inside the hoods of our sweatshirts, we all would loiter, holding up the walls, smoking a little weed, talking shit, listening to hip-hop and making plans to be big somewhere and somehow. My boom box was always there, providing the sounds. NWA's *Straight Outta Compton* was the shit.

The old ladies in the building were all scared of the odorous smells and aggressive sounds of young boys with no direction. They repeatedly called the police on us. That meant Moms would have to take time off of work to come and get me. She questioned how many times she would have to come get me out for smoking weed. I felt bad for her having to come and get me. She *couldn't* make sure that I wouldn't do it, smoke weed, and I didn't stop.

The primal beats of our music and the harsh words that we sang reverberated throughout the building, shaking the walls and rattling frail nerves. Our favorite joint was "Fuck the Police" and we knew all the words.

We sipped our 40s and smoked our blunts, getting higher and higher.

There was still no hiding for me. My Moms always dreaded hearing the sound of my gruff, scratchy voice in the hallway when she came home from work after twelve thirty a.m. My unusual voice had always been like that, but smoking all that weed probably made it deeper and even more distinct.

In the hallways, Moms could hear me and spoke softly to me into the darkness. "Jeff, is that you?" I would sink deeper into the folds of my sweatshirt, hoping that she would just go upstairs and go to bed.

I was just a kid that was doing what he saw others doing.

*

June 20, 2011

The weekend done came and went and it's now Tuesday. I had fun this weekend on TRF. We're allowed to stay up til 2 AM and 6 AM on Saturday. I dubbed it Club Oneida LOL. We stayed up both nights, me and Q, Smitty, JB and Pito, talking about life and watching movies and shooting the shit. They're good dudes. It's kinda hard to write on the weekends being that we stay up so late. I be tired as hell but it helps pass the time. Me and Hank been busting ass in spades. I haven't lost yet. I'm the champ around here. Ha Ha. I've been speaking to Ish and the kids every day. They all came to see me this weekend along with my Mom, minus Britt. She has her acting classes on Saturday and I don't want her to miss it so I'll be seeing her on Sundays. I was worried about Lil Rule taking this situation hard, but now I'm worried about Britt, she seems to be taking it the hardest. I love them all so much and these are such critical years for a young girl growing up. She really needs her Dad right now and me not being there hurts but she's strong and I know she'll get through it. Times like these build character and you need a good support system to get through.

I was tired as hell on Sunday, going on my visit fuckin wit these inmates all night. We're like little kids sneaking around, for me to get my haircut so I could look half way decent on my visit. Smitty played lookout, smoking cigarettes in the dayroom and then blowing the smoke into the vents so we don't get caught while the C.O.'s are in the bubble. LOL. We also hid bread so we could have extra to make our meals. It's real high school shit. LOL. But fun Nonetheless. Saturday we watched a couple of good movies, Inception *and* Animal. *While watching* Animal *we all were touched by a dose of reality, because we realized that we're all young Black men caught up in an ugly cycle that's been going on for generations—the Willie Lynch Syndrome—which made me mad at myself for still playing my part in this fucked up game. We all felt stupid as we watched, knowing we were right where society wanted us, in jail away from our family and kids. It's hard to break the cycle when we're not there to teach our sons to be men and our daughters to be women. As I sit behind these walls I'm learning that life is not a game, it's a reality show and every episode is a learning experience, where hopefully you get that second season to right your wrongs after you've made a fool of yourself. It's easy to make excuses, but at the end of the day, it all boils down to the decisions you make. I've made some bad choices in my life, some that could have landed me in here for life. God looks out for children and fools. Lord knows I'm not a child anymore and I promise this will be the last time I play the fool. I started work today, they got me doing lawns and grounds in the morn, then Porter work in the afternoons. It gets me out this fuckin cell. At least it's not hard work and it gets me outside during the day before rec. time. I haven't started school yet, but everyone says that shit is a joke and that the teacher never comes. Shit, Steve been here 4 years and still hasn't got his GED. He gets out in 2 days and now they are telling him he has to get it on the outside. But we can lift weights all day—that's right niggas use your brawn and not your brain. LOL. God forbid we educate you to break the cycle. Education is a good thing. I like to read and write. I don't need that good enough diploma. I was smart enough to make millions of dollars, but it would be nice to have a diploma so when I'm preaching education to my kids they can't say, "Well, you don't have a diploma and made out just fine." We all know having talent and actually making good use of it is the luck of the draw no matter how hard you work. You know how many talented motherfuckers are working at Walmart. LOL. It's not what you know it's who you know. I started reading this book by Sista Souljah called* Midnight and the Meaning of Love. *It's a good book that got a lot of jewels in it. I'm glad to see that she didn't let the politricks of this bullshit industry discourage her. She's using her pen in a mightier way than she ever could by rapping. Not to say she wasn't a good rapper but kids don't wanna hear that conscious shit in music, they wanna be entertained. I've also been hittin the weights pretty hard. I'm about 165 right now. I plan on leaving this bitch at about 190. They gonna think I was in here lifting Toyotas. LOL. All in all, jail is a place you never wanna be, but it's also a place that is unique. I never would've become one wit myself on the streets because there are too many temptations and distractions. It's sad but some of the greatest thoughts were sparked right here in prison.*

*

THREE

———

Hard Breathing

I WAS STANDING AT THE FRONT DOOR OF MY CRIB AND THERE it was—an eviction notice. *We've moved six times in two years.* There was nothing I could do except take it off the door and give it to Moms. She was inside getting ready for work. I slowly handed the notice to her and she looked at it with tears welling in her eyes. She sat down at the kitchen table with her head in her hands. The sight of Moms' hands shielding her shame tore me up. I hadn't seen her cry like that since my father was in the house.

All I could whisper to her was, "It's going to be okay, Moms. It's going to be okay." It was up to me to make sure that it *was.* I'd always been a fighter, even though I was one of the smaller dudes on the block. Moms once told me when I was in second grade, "Jeff, you have to *fight* to survive. They should never let your size fool them. If someone hits you, you better hit them back."

And that's what I was going to do.

MOMS AND ME were the Black Sheep of the family, for real, so we couldn't turn to family. Luckily, my Moms had good friends. We went to stay with one of her male friends who lived in Rochdale Village. Rochdale was one of those high-rise co-ops that tower over Queens, looking a lot like the projects but it wasn't considered one. Rochdale Village has twenty different buildings in five groups. Each building has three sections, A, B or C, and each floor has about fifteen apartments. Even though RV *wasn't* the projects, it was notorious for its drug activity. I could see that there were a lot of customers to serve and money to get.

In high school money and music were starting to weigh heavily on my brain. The chorus from KRS-One's song kept tickling me: *love's gonna get'cha . . . love's gonna get'cha. . . .* Love *had* gotten me; I loved my Moms and I needed to rescue her. The things that I wanted like fly sneakers, new gear or three-finger rings, Moms could never afford. But now with the eviction, our needs were *serious*. I decided to take myself out of the equation by making my own money. The music kept daring me as I walked through the hectic streets of Queens with only one foot in school and the other chasing hip-hop. "Love's Gonna Get'cha (Material Love)" was constantly in my head.

I pull about a G, a week. Fuck school.

But it was the chorus that made up my mind.

Tell me what the fuck am I supposed to do?

Hell yeah.

Moms was still working the four-to-twelve shift. It seemed like she was always working, so I couldn't really understand why we got evicted. Moms struggled with money like everyone else in the hood. I didn't see her much anymore because of her work and social life. In her absence, I hung with my homies on 1-9-1 every chance I got. That was a lot of fuck-off time for me. All I could see and hear were homies talking about getting money quick, if and when they needed it.

All my homies and me did was smoke weed and talk a lot of shit and get into trouble. My teachers didn't really like me much because they didn't understand Black kids. They certainly didn't understand *me*. They had all decided that I was a troublemaker, which I probably was. I was one of those guys whose favorite subject was gym, and the teachers judged me for it. I was good at math and science, too, but I was more interested in writing rhymes.

Looking back, I wish I had paid more attention in English class. I didn't know then that reading poetry would have been the same as writing rhymes. Reading short stories and novels would have been the same as constructing the storylines in my music.

I had started carrying my lyric book because after writing rhymes on scraps of paper I needed more space. My composition book was empty and it was the perfect size for me to write rhymes in. I carried it wherever I went, constantly scribbling and making sense of shit on paper.

> *I'm going to show this world my struggle, my pain, my hunger,*
> *my hustle . . .*

That lyric kept going through my head. I wrote the line down and let it sit for a while until the next line eventually came to me. Thinking about Kristen, I knew I should feel lucky to be alive, but I also knew that life was full of struggle, pain and hunger.

IN SPEAKING OF life and death, this reminds me of some things that happened in junior high school. It went like this . . . "Yo. Peep this," is what Harold would whisper to Jason and me. His lips trembled as he tried to hide his excitement. His look was a signal for us to follow him down the hall to where his locker was. Harold brought a gun to school. Harold would open his heavy bag carefully and the gun would shine from the bottom like sunshine in the ghetto. The piece was smooth and black. After Jason and I gawked at the thing long enough, Harold would casually throw a book and some papers on top of it, zip up the bag and bounce. We would be left standing there to think about that gun for the rest of the day.

I wanted to see it again. I wanted to hold it. Feel it in my fingers. Bear the weight. Pull the trigger, even. Once I got introduced to guns, I hungered for the rush of power that only a man with a gun has.

Harold's uncles were in the drug game and that's where he got the gun. According to Harold, his uncles had everything they would ever need: guns, drugs, women and money. Harold loved to brag about that shit.

In junior high school I spent most of my weekends at my man Jason's house in Laurelton. He had a nice-sized house with a big basement that Jason made into a little world that was just for us. He even had a private entrance. We would use the basement door to bring girls in and out. Jason's sister was in college and so it was just him and his Moms in that big old house. Jason didn't have a father, like the rest of us. His mother, Ms. LeGrand, never came down the stairs. She gave us *space* and we loved her for that. She would deal with us from the top of the stairs, only.

"Boys! There's food in the refrigerator," or "I'm going out. Boys, remember to do the right thing!" she would yell down as she left the house. And we would all laugh at what we thought was the right thing versus what Ms. LeGrand thought.

Jason's basement felt like a sprawling luxury condominium. It had different rooms. One had the couches and the TV, the next room had beds in it. There was another small room where we would take turns cutting each other's hair, making our flat tops as flat as we could get them. There was even a cellar door where we could sit on the steps and smoke weed. We would blow the smoke out of the cracks so the smell wouldn't come in. We knew that Ms. LeGrand wasn't coming down, but just in case. . . .

We got into some shenanigans around our way. I masterminded much crazy shit. One of our favorite things to do was going to the Chinese joint and ordering our favorites: pork fried rice, chicken wings, extra ketchup and extra hot sauce. We would always run out with the food, without paying. The little Chinese man would be yelling and screaming after us, but he could never catch us. Chinese people *hated* Black people. We didn't give a fuck. We laughed as we ran out the door, singing "Fuck the Police." That NWA shit was dope. We loved that radical shit. Fuck the police, for real. We wanted the Chinese man to know that we weren't scared even if he did call them on us.

Eventually, we needed new stuff to do. We started ordering pizzas and holding up the pizza man. We needed a gun if we were going to stick up the pizza man, the right way, getting money and pizza! Harold hooked us up without a problem. We didn't even have to pay him. He said we could use the .38 pistol whenever we needed it. It was just enough heat to get what we wanted without the problems.

Ms. LeGrand was devoutly Christian and the only way that she would let Jason have friends sleep over was if we all went to church with her on Sunday mornings. We would all drag ourselves out of the cots in the basement on Sunday mornings after a night of weed smoking and talking much shit. Our bellies were full of stolen Chinese food and our eyes sagged, heavy with lack of sleep. We regularly took a trip to Pop and Kims to get Old English and we drank as many of those extra-cold 40s as we could carry. The Chinese man who owned the store never asked us for identification. All that mattered was that he got his money.

We all kept our wrinkled church clothes stashed behind the couch in a plastic grocery store bag. Ms. LeGrand never said anything about how wrinkled we all looked. When she passed us, she would only show her concern by pulling on our wrinkled shirttails, reminding us to tuck in our shirts and checking to see if we had belts on. She would tell us to stand up straight and then she would smile like we were all something to be proud of.

On Sunday mornings, Ms. LeGrand would stand tall beside us crumpled boys. She looked regal as a queen. Her perfume smelled of baby powder and soap.

It was fun at Jason's house, I ain't gonna lie. The troubles in my head seemed to melt away when I was chilling with him and the crew. Going to church with Ms. LeGrand was *way* better than going to Kingdom Hall. I didn't really mind church. I could have fun and chill with the fellas and still be with God for a few hours each week.

After the disfellowshipping of Moms, I realized that I wasn't really religious, either. Being raised a Jehovah's Witness showed me that religion was about having a middleman and going to church is to make people feel better about themselves. I could see what it did for Ms. LeGrand. After the Witnesses treated Moms and me so ill, I knew I never wanted a middleman to get between God and me, again. I never needed to hear someone tell me to love God. *I just do.* I didn't want no one to tell me to put my money in a basket. Hell, I didn't have no money, anyway.

I REALLY DON'T think that KRS-One was deliberately trying to get me to start selling drugs but his video was telling the story of my life and the life of everyone that looked like me. The video showed a kid in junior high school, like me, who was trying to do the right thing like doing a bullshit paper route to make money. His Moms was broke, his sister had wack clothes, the family was eating bread, beans and rice and he was the *joke* of the neighborhood until the neighborhood drug dealer showed him the way. The drug dealer had a fly car, a cell phone, cash and guns. When the drug dealer invited the kid to do just one "drop," suddenly the kid was eating *steak* with his beans and rice. His sister finally got some fresh gear and shit all worked out in the end.

So tell me what the fuck am I supposed to do?

I HAD BECOME CURIOUS about selling drugs. Our first foray into selling was in junior high school. Jason, Kavin and I started putting chunks of Ivory soap into crack vials and selling them for five dollars. We would shave the pieces off of a bar of Ivory soap with a sharp knife. It looked like crack. We were just trying to make a little money to get enough for food and 40s. We were not trying to sell drugs or make big money. We were happy when we made fifty dollars.

We were still playing it safe in Laurelton, around Jason's crib, which was a little less hardcore than around my way. It was the suburbs, for real. We really thought the soap thing was just harmless mischief. When the fiends around Jason's way started to complain about the shit they had just bought, one of the older hustlers stepped to us.

"What the fuck are you little niggas doing? You're fucking up my block. If you're going to do this shit, then keep it *real* with something that niggas *want* to buy. Get some real dope, not no bullshit."

That scared us, a little. We stopped doing the soap thing for a minute. Besides, we knew that when we were ready to keep it real, it would be easier back on my block, because I knew all the dudes running it.

Even Moms' brother, my Uncle Dennis, who was five years older than me, was out there. Dennis worked for Kurt, who was short and chubby and drove a BMW 325. He was a good dude who got shot in his own house. Uncle Dennis always insisted that I was too young to be hustling. Losing Kurt had been hard on him and he wanted to keep me out of the dangerous shit. I resented that when he said it because I felt that he was trying to block me from getting mine, even though he was getting his. *Fuck that.* I would just get mine somewhere else.

My man Black was also in the game. Chris Black was one of the homies from Hollis. He was a tall dark guy with a low fade and an imposing presence. He was always a prankster and he liked to rhyme, too. He and I were cool.

During high school, I even checked out the burglary thing for a minute. I wasn't really into it, though. I probably did it two or three times. In home invasions, I *could* get a gang of shit: cash, jewelry, tape recorders, which all had some street value, but I could see the unnecessary risks involved. I got my hands on some gate cutters, which we used to use to cut gates and locks and shit in order to bomb the buildings that had the cleanest walls. We were on to some next-level petty crimes.

I remember one day when I was skipping school. I was chilling on my fire escape, getting high. I had been writing in my lyric book and then took a break to smoke. When I got on my fire escape, I looked up. I saw a muthafucka coming down the fire escape after climbing out of a window above me. I was just about to tell that muthafucka to get the fuck outta here, when I recognized him. It was Champ's little brother, L'il D.

"What's up, nigga," I said.

"Yo, nigga. I just lifted some shit from the crib upstairs."

"Word?" My curiosity was piqued. "Wait for me." I wasn't even trying to rob a house that day. I went inside to get my shoes on so we could climb back up there to see if we could find any more good shit. When we got up there, L'il D was wrong. It wasn't much left in there. It was just some petty shit like a hair dryer and an old pager.

You see, robbing houses just wasn't my thing. I would rather work for my money. If you get caught robbing houses you'd get hit serving time and all you really got out of it was some trinkets such as watches or maybe if you're lucky, a gold chain. It was *bullshit* for all that trouble. I would rather sell drugs any day and get a hard $300 in cash and know exactly what I was getting into. Robbing houses involved too many guessing games. I didn't want to *hope* I would get something out of a deal. I wanted to know for sure. To me, hustling was a better bet.

When he and I got back down the fire escape, I let him out of the front door of my crib and went back to working on the rhyme that I had started. All I had was the chorus and the title: "Race Against Time."

In my race against time I—can't stop
Runnin through the red light—livin my life

Even if I'm gettin too high
I'mma keep runnin through the red light—livin my life

I WAS ALWAYS HIGH as a kite. Moms knew it. She smelled it. She saw my bloodshot, watery eyes. She hadn't asked me much about it since those nights she would find me in the hall with my homies, when I first came back to live with her. Whenever Moms was at work, I was smoking in the house with my friends, all the time. I used a fan to blow the smoke out of the window, but Moms could still detect it. Finally, she decided to ask me about it one day.

"Jeffrey, are you smoking weed?" I was fourteen years old. What was I going to say? She saw all of the chips and cookie bags strewn all over the house. She could also never wake me up in the morning for school. Whenever she would come home from work, my homie Aaron and I were sprawled out on the floor with the TV watching us. I couldn't deny it.

"Yes, Ma, I been smoking, please don't trip," I confessed.

"If you're going to smoke, I guess I can't stop you. You need to stay away from the police. I don't trust 'em. They don't care about boys like you. They'll shoot you for no reason. And, they laugh when they get away with it."

Too bad my father left eight years before. He might have handled that shit differently. Even though he was struggling with addiction himself, maybe just the sound of his voice would have scared me a little more than Moms' feminine voice did. Maybe his tone would have inspired me to do the right thing when I was going down the wrong path. I sometimes imagined what it would be like to just have him around. But mostly, during that period I felt having him around would do more harm than good. That made me think, *Fuck him, I don't need him.*

Moms shook her head. "I can't keep going to the police station with you over this stuff." She stood there for a minute, not knowing what her next move should be. Finally, she said, "Okay. You can smoke in the house. Just stay off the streets and out of the hallways."

You give young men an inch and they take a yard. I *pushed.* "You know, Ma, smoking is a social thing. It's not fun to smoke alone."

She sighed. "You can have one or two friends here to smoke with you. No more than two. If I catch you with more than two boys in here, that'll be it. I'll stop it all! I mean it, Jeff!"

It was worth going to school the next day because at three p.m., I would be able to say, "Well, niggas, I'm going to catch a smoke."

"Where at?" Mike would ask.

"Home, nigga, where you think?"

"Your Moms knows you smoke in the crib?" Aaron would wonder.

"My Moms is mad cool, yo," I'd say, nonchalantly. My mom was smarter than that—she was concerned with keeping me out of jail, out of trouble and off the streets.

You have to have something to brag about when shit is all fucked-up.

There's no way I would have tried this if a man like Grandpa Cherry was in the picture.

I WAS STILL CURIOUS about the drug thing. Nothing much had changed except I was not doing well in high school because I was smoking weed and cutting classes. When we were still staying with my mom's friend in RV, I could see how much paper there was to get. And, we still needed money. I knew hustling may be the ticket.

My man Mike put me on by introducing me to Little B, who hit me off with my first pack. A pack consisted of twenty rocks valued at about $100. I didn't know what to do with that shit but I knew that when I figured it out, I would get money and be able to get us out of a bad situation. I was the man of the house now.

My first time on the block, I was terrible out there. When I started hustling, I saw that everyone out there already had regular customers. I had to work hard to get my own. And, nobody tried to help me, either. It took me a whole week to move that one pack.

I wasn't being hooked up with any customers. I had to go out and get the stragglers who were unestablished customers and were as new to the game as I was. I had to be aggressive to get them, which was risky, too. It's not cool to go out there trying to sell to muthafuckas you don't know. They could be police.

Standing on the corner on those cold blistery days, I learned to observe people in new ways. I would be all bundled up with my hat pulled close over my head, so that my ears would not burn with the cold. Only my eyes were visible and I was using them to detect who was real and who could be a trap. Regular customers had longer conversations. They would spend time asking for discounts, cutting deals and setting up payment arrangements. The cops, on the other hand, always tried to act like real customers, so they were stiff and brief, which was a dead giveaway. I was watching as hard as I could and slowly catching on.

When someone would approach me, I would say to them, "Let's go around this corner and let me see you smoke that shit right here." If they were real, they would do whatever I asked them to do to get a smoke. It always worked.

Once I figured out how to get customers, the game was relatively simple from what I could see. There were nickels, dimes and twenties. Nickels cost five dollars. Dimes, ten dollars, and twenties, twenty dollars. One rock would get the fiends high for a very short time. Crack is a short high, that's why it was such a big hustle. Our job was to get them high so they would want more . . . within the hour.

I first tried to work for a guy named BG. He was a little flashy dude, but he was getting money, though. Then, there was Black, who was one of my first lieutenants in the game and still one of my best friends.

School was becoming a problem. It was getting harder and harder to get real money and go to school at the same time. I couldn't get regular customers if I wasn't standing on my corner. It was as simple as that.

The school started calling my house in the afternoon. Moms was already gone to work and I was on the block, hustling. They couldn't catch up with her or me. To me, school was the place to go to further yourself in order to make money. Since I was making money already, I figured, what did I need with school? I had found my route to the money and I needed to focus on that.

Moms could see that something was up with me. When homies would come to my crib, we were always up, laughing and roughhousing late into the night, long after Moms got home. She was especially suspicious when Aaron, a kid from John Adams High School, was over so much. My man Aaron was a year older than me, always on time, always at school and got good grades. Everyone thought that Aaron was a good kid. Until he met me.

Aaron liked being down with me on those late nights in my crib when we were getting high.

When he got a settlement from a car accident, he got his own car, a Nissan Maxima. After that, it was a no-brainer. He was *the* one to hang with. When Aaron and I started hanging out more than before, he kept his grades up, until he could no longer be a good guy and a cool guy at the same time.

THROUGH THE DENSE cloud of weed smoke, the fire of hip-hop and learning to hustle, my worlds somehow collided. I got arrested on my first gun charge with my homies and Aaron.

My man E-Funk from around Cherry's house came to get us in the morning at my crib in his pop's old Buick. It was morning and I was starving. We decided to go to IHOP for breakfast before we started hustling. I suggested that we load the car with all of the shit so we didn't have to make two trips. Aaron didn't agree with me but they all went along with what I said, anyway. We loaded up the car with our two guns and the drugs.

The funny shit is we never even got to IHOP. On the way there, we turned down a side street to park the car. The cops were on that street, arresting someone else. My homie O had pulled onto the block and then he reversed out of it suddenly, jerking the car. We started going the other way.

"Shit!" O said. We all froze.

"Why did you do that?" I said. "That was stupid! You think they didn't see that shit?"

"Yeah, man, you should have just kept going!" Aaron moaned.

Within a few seconds, we could see the cops' lights in the rearview mirror.

O pulled over. I knew that the cops would find the weed and the guns. I could feel my heart beating fast in my chest. My homie Dirt threw one of the guns into an empty lot before the cops got to us. Everyone had started sprinkling drugs all over the car. I was the only person who kept my drugs on my person. The cops searched the car. They were homicide police so they didn't really care about the drugs or the fact that the car was stolen. Guns was what they were looking for.

"Get out of the car," a policeman said to us.

Me, Dirt, Aaron and O slowly pulled ourselves out of the car. As we were positioning ourselves in a line so they could search us, Dirt just shot off like a bullet, running as fast as he could into the street and around the corner. Dirt was a chunky dude. It was funny to see him moving fast, carrying the extra weight. I smiled to myself just knowing that Dirt had taken the one gun that was left in the car. But I was wrong. Dirt was scared as shit, and had forgotten about the gun. It was still in the car to be found by the cops. The cops found the crack on me, too.

Dirt ran, in the snow, and hid under a car for four hours.

As we were taken down to the station to be booked, Black went over to Moms' house. We didn't have a home phone then. Moms had to get in touch with Aaron's moms, who couldn't believe it.

It worked out for most of us. Aaron didn't get anything except for an earful from his moms. Since it was his first time getting in trouble, his moms was freaking the fuck out. All she could do was cry and repeat, "How did *you* get involved with *these* boys?"

My Moms was getting heated at his moms. "What are you trying to say? Your son is no better than mine."

Aaron's moms turned to him but spoke for us all to hear, "Aaron, I can't believe it, I can't believe it. This is not like *you!*"

Aaron and O got off with no probation.

My case went before the judge. I was ROR'd, released on my own recognizance, as a person with no priors. I was given five years' probation and one hundred hours of community service. I got probation because I was a youthful offender.

But someone still had to take the weight for the remaining gun that was found. E-Funk had drug priors, he was eighteen years old *and* he had stolen his parents' car that night. The thing that's not fair about the system is that if one person didn't claim the gun, we would have all been charged for it. Since E-Funk could not make bail, he took it. His parents refused to come down to the station to pay the bail. E-Funk ended up serving one year, which was time served, for the gun charge.

I was assigned to janitorial work at a fine arts center on Jamaica Avenue in Queens. The lady who was in charge of the center didn't really want offenders on the premises, even though she signed up for the program and enjoyed the tax breaks it offered. She thought the art patrons would be afraid to come to the center if they saw a bunch of criminals in there. The couple of times that I reported to work, Linda, the blond fat lady, signed me in and signed me out at the same time. She would say, "Mr. Jeffrey, you are free to go!"

After "working" there, my community service detail was switched to cleaning parks and collecting trash from the side of the highway. I met some cool guys there. One of them was so wild that he started bringing weed. We smoked it while we picked up the garbage and the COs waited just a few feet away. But I should have realized that this whole thing was just the beginning. It was a warning, but just not strong enough.

*

June 28, 2011

*Today is Lil Rules Birthday, and I'm SICK that I'm not there
to share it with him. These times will no doubt be the hardest—
birthdays, holidays. I still can't believe I'm in Fucking Prison!
I'm sad, hurt, angry all in one, but I can't let my emotions get the
best of me. I gotta stay calm, cool, collected so that everyone else
does the same. I need to be strong and Ish been holding up well
minus some occasional tears, but that's to be understood given the
circumstances.*

    *Rule turns 11 today, and as I sit in my cell writing this I can't
help noticing my state greens with my inmate number staring at
me 11R2024. The 11R sticks out like a fuckin omen or something,
as if it's screaming you fuckin asshole. I've been having a lot of
dreams lately, all of which have been family oriented, some a lil
weird. LOL. But all of them darkened by the reality of when I
awake. I'm still here locked in a cell and even my breath of fresh
air is guarded by barbed wire fences. I feel trapped. But my dreams
set me free for a moment. They feel so real I don't wanna wake
up. I just wanna be home with my sons and my daughter and my
wife and my mother. But I'm 19 months short of that dream. I
keep a picture of me and my wife taped to my locker right above*

my head. It's a newspaper clipping of the day I turned myself in. My mother and Ish's mom and Gutta are also in the background. I keep it as a constant reminder of the mistakes I've made and as I sit here on my son's birthday I can't help but to think about the next newspaper clipping I'll keep. The one when I'm walking out.

Happy Birthday Jeffrey B. Atkins Jr.

I LOVE YOU.

*

FOUR

—

Soulmates

I WAS LATE AGAIN TO EIGHTH-GRADE SHOP CLASS. I ACTUALLY liked shop class because we were learning how to do other things with our hands besides rolling blunts, tilting 40s and lifting things that didn't belong to us. When I rolled into class there was a new girl sitting in the front row. They said that she had just moved to Queens from Atlanta, Georgia. My eye was drawn to her as soon as I saw her. She was cute. She had long shiny hair and a pretty smile. I walked over to her and said hi.

She said hi back to me but didn't seem very interested. Kavin and Devin were still my homies. We used to hang out with a few girls that we were tight with. The new girl from Atlanta was already hanging with them, too. Soon, she was hanging out with all of us. She was real cute so it wasn't a surprise that the other girls wanted to be friends with her. Aisha could pull the guys because she was new and she was fly.

The new girl was already seeing Devin before I could even make a move on her. Her name was Aisha Fatima Murray. Aisha's voice didn't sound like she was from Atlanta. I was expecting her to have that slow, polite drawl and a too-sweet smile on her face. Instead, she sounded a lot like the girls from around the way. She was nice and all but I could tell that she was not a pushover. I liked that. I wanted to know more but I couldn't disrespect my man Devin so I chilled.

After school we all would walk around the neighborhood, laughing and talking and getting our daily after-school pizza at the Pizza Hut right on the corner. Devin and I were the clowns of the group. We were always making the girls laugh. We did impressions of our teachers and skits about church, making fun of the ministers.

"Haaaalleluuuu-jah," I would bellow in my best preacher's voice. I seemed to make Aisha laugh the most but I had to be careful that I didn't upset Devin. The crew had a pact that we didn't mess with girls that someone in the crew was already dealing with.

Even though I was young, I was already very interested in sex, like every boy at that age. There were lots of girls that I had gotten with since losing my virginity at eleven in the stairwell of the Woodhull projects.

One Saturday, Devin and I were in the park enjoying a summer day, when we saw Aisha. Devin and Aisha had already broken up during the school year.

I could recognize Aisha's long, shiny black hair anywhere. She was one of the few girls in the neighborhood that had hair like that. She was walking with her little sister, Antoinette.

"Whatcha doing?" I walked up to Aisha.

"Going to see my grandmother," she said as if she was hoping that I had a better suggestion.

"Wanna come hang out later at the crib?"

Later that day after she went to check on her grandmother, Aisha and her girl Alicia came to see us.

When they arrived, Aisha and Devin were still cool with each other. The four of us were giddy that day. Devin and I were high already, which made everything funny as shit. We were always full of stories from school. *Did you see what she was wearing? Did you hear what he did? Are they going to get suspended for that shit?*

Devin and Alicia hooked up that night and I figured it was cool for me to kick it with Aisha. Aisha became my girl. And I liked that. I had heard a lot of the older guys talking about having one steady chick and I wanted to experience that feeling. There were lots of girls checking for me. I had already been through many girls. Sometimes I wanted to have someone else to talk to besides my homies. I wanted to have a girlfriend who was always there for me and who had my back.

Aisha was originally from Queens until a friend of her mother's told her that Atlanta was a good place to move. In Atlanta, there were jobs and affordable housing. *Nice, big* houses, they had told her. Aisha had two sisters, Antoinette and Kenya, and all three of them had a different father.

Aisha and I had been through the same types of things. And when we saw each other, she would tell me all the things that were bottled up inside her and needed to be said. Most of the time, she would talk about her confused feelings, the father she never knew and why her mother had so many problems. I always found myself listening and thinking, *Me too.*

Aisha's smile receded when she talked about her time in Atlanta. "We were only there for a few months when moms realized that Atlanta was not the right place, after all."

She paused and then continued, "Both of my sisters' fathers came to Atlanta to get them. Kenya went to Buffalo, New York, to live with her father and Antoinette was brought back to Queens to live with her grandmother." Then, she added slowly, "Except for mine . . . I was stranded in Atlanta with my Aunt Gerry, while my moms went back to Queens to try to get her old job back."

There was silence and then Aisha said one last thing. "My moms was always *struggling.* We were always needing family members to help us out."

"Me too," I said quietly.

"Don't you just hate that? It was more than one time that we had to go through that shit," she said. She closed her eyes and her forehead wrinkled.

Me too, I thought, but I just listened to her stories, which sounded more and more like my own. We were both looking at life through the same smudged lenses.

AT THE END of the summer things were changing because we were all entering high school. Aisha and Harold went to Martin Van Buren High School and I went to John Adams High School on the South Side. John Adams was a little rougher than Van Buren. There was a neighborhood riff between Hollis and the South Side. John Adams was on the South Side and so it was an audacious choice for me to choose to go all the way to John Adams when I was from Hollis, but I was fearless.

I didn't want to go to Van Buren because Uncle Dennis was a senior there and I wanted to make my own mark. I didn't want to be seen as Dennis' "little brother." I wanted to go to Adams, to be in a place where no one knew my name.

Things between Aisha and me were changing, too. We broke up. I still had a lot of girls checking me. There were no hard feelings between Aisha and me. We stayed friends and saw each other in the neighborhood almost every day.

I was hanging out with Devin's older brother, Chuck, a lot more than before. Chuck and I were both in the game, while Devin had started to get serious about basketball, so we didn't hang out as much anymore. In junior high school Devin and I played in all the tournaments. Although I was cool at basketball, I was too small to make it big. Chuck was down when I started hustling. It was natural that we would become friends.

Hanging with Chuck was all about learning the game and getting new experiences. The first experience I got with Chuck I would never forget. Chuck took me to see his girl, who had a roommate. Drug dealers were a hot commodity among young girls in the hood.

Because Chuck was older than me, he knew older girls. Although I had come very far since the stairwell at Woodhull, Chuck put me on to the real deal. Chuck's girl had a cute roommate who had smooth brown skin and a short Halle Berry haircut. It was crazy how shit went down between us, but I figured that's how the older kids rolled. "Halle" took me into her bedroom and did it to me, without me ever knowing her name or her knowing mine. She had a curvy woman's body and she knew exactly what to do with hers and mine, too.

"Halle" and I started to kiss as we took off each other's clothes. It was like how I'd wanted sex to be: butt-naked bodies, heavy breathing and sweaty skin rubbing up against everywhere. We took our time and enjoyed each other. It was not the rushed "kid" sex. *Now that's what I am talking about.*

I still saw Aisha around the way and out on the street when I was out there hustling. Her grandmother lived across from the park that we all hung out in. Aisha had a boyfriend and I had several girls that I saw, but none of them were serious. Whenever I saw Aisha, we would speak to each other and every time she walked away, I would think how much I wished I could've talked to her a little longer. But we were moving in different directions—or so I thought.

She was a sweet girl and I was a drug dealer. The truth is, all of the chicks around my way had a man who sold drugs. We were the only kind of guys around and some of the big-time hustlers even had cars. Aisha was no fool. She wanted what all the other girls had, so her new boyfriend at her new school hustled, too.

CHUCK, MIKE AND I had gotten into the habit of cutting school in high school. We would go for a few periods, lounge in the lunchroom and then we'd bounce. Lucky for us, the security guard, Luther, who guarded the side door smoked crack. Luther had a Jheri curl and a bad lisp. We used to see that fiend after school at Rochdale Village. After we saw him once, we had the dirt on him. We made an agreement that we would sell him crack at a discounted rate in exchange for easy access in and out of the school's side door. Luther was happy to go along. Sometimes ten of us would leave school at the same time to go chill at the park, roll some dice and then go back to school. Or, we would get something to eat and then come back through that door.

"WHAT'S UP WITH CHERYL? Have you seen her recently?" Mike asked me one day.

"Nah. Let's call them and see what they up to?" I said to Mike. Aisha and I were still friends and I knew that Mike was really feeling Aisha's cousin, Cheryl.

"Hey, Jeff. What are you guys doing for New Year's Eve?"

"Nothing, what's up, girl?" I said.

"I'm having a party. Wanna come?"

"Who's going to be there?" I asked for Mike.

"Are you with Mike?" Aisha didn't pull no punches.

"Who wants to know?"

"Tell him that Cheryl will be there. Bring him."

"Bet."

AT THE PARTY, Aisha and I talked a lot. We realized that we should not have broken up at the beginning of ninth grade. We were in the eleventh grade at that point and the time seemed right for us to try again.

Things with Aisha fell right back into place. We saw each other as often as we could. I was a hustler also trying to do music. We'd hang out at the park, go out to eat and talk on the phone. One day when we were walking, I got my nerve up. "Listen to my new verse. It's called 'Story to Tell.'" Aisha sat on the park bench and I stood away from her and closed my eyes so I could imagine the beat. Then, I spit the verse that I was working on:

Listen up, I got a story to tell
On the streets we got guns and drugs for sale
Cause you hos know the game that we play is real
Keep your mind on the money and your weapons concealed

"*Sounds dope.* When can I hear the rest?" she said.

That was the most positive thing I'd heard about my music from anyone besides my homies. Cherry used to call it "bippity bop" music and he always said it was not real work and it never would be. Aisha believed in me more than I believed in myself.

"It's not finished yet, but when I do, I'll let you check it out," I promised.

My lyrics didn't scare Aisha. She knew the deal. Aisha was no stranger to the streets and that's why she was the girl for me. No matter what happened, or what I would eventually share with Aisha about my life, she could relate.

WHEN I MET AISHA'S MOMS, I recognized her. She used to see me on the block. Her moms used to mess with one of the guys that I hustled for. Sometimes she spoke to me and sometimes she didn't. Sometimes, neither one of us wanted to be recognized, being where we were and doing what we were doing.

"You know, I worry about you, baby," Aisha said to me often. I hadn't heard that from anyone except from my Moms and Grandma Cherry, years before. But when Aisha said it, it sounded different. It made me feel that it may be safe to love her. I liked her. I wanted more of Aisha than I was getting. She and I were getting close but getting to the sex felt like an eternity. We hadn't gotten there—yet.

I never pressured Aisha because I felt that she was worth waiting for. She and I had lots of sexy fun together even though we weren't having actual sex. She was affectionate and made me feel solid, like she and I were going to be together, always. There was just no me without her. It was just the way she held my hand when we walked.

THE ETERNITY was finally over.

"I love you," Aisha said to me as I kissed her forehead and held her tight.

I didn't say it, but I was thinking, *Me too.*

I grew up without birthdays or Christmas so being with Aisha in this way felt like a Christmas gift that I'd been waiting to unwrap my whole life. She was sixteen and I was seventeen. I'd been trying to get with her like this for two years. Feeling her silky skin beneath me was like nothing I'd ever felt before. It wasn't about me taking something from her or her giving me something. We were turning into *us.* I could feel my heart for the first time in years. Aisha was not like the other girls, she was everything.

MOMS AND I were on completely different shifts. She was never around. I'd barely made it to the eleventh grade. Although I was struggling to finish, my interest in school was totally gone. I had money and music on my mind. I thought that the shit they were teaching in school had nothing to do with my life. I used to think, fuck history and social studies. But I was *wrong*. If we don't know our history, we are lost. This is most definitely true for Black men. We need to be constantly reminded of the great men that have come before us or we'll believe what the TV says about us. The images on the screen rarely make us feel good about ourselves, rarely inspire us to do meaningful shit.

Moms was on the night shift, four to two, and I was working a morning shift. Moms had lost track of me and didn't realize why my heart was no longer in school. As with all mothers, she wanted better for me. She really wanted me to graduate from high school.

My lyric notebook was filling up. I had written hundreds of rhymes, some that were going to be hits if I could just get them out there.

IN HIGH SCHOOL, my homies started calling me Left because of the knockout game. The object of the game was to see who could knock out a crackhead with a single punch. I guess my homies and me were actually the only ones playing the game. The crackheads were like our game pieces. The crackheads were always fucked-up, stumbling down the street like wide-eyed zombies. They would swerve from side to side as they approached us trying to get some crack for free. We were weeded-up, too, and everything was topsy-turvy. Everything was funny as hell. If the crackhead would sway to the left, I would hit him from the right with a left. The fiends couldn't even see our punches coming and then with one light tap, BAM! they were out cold laying on the ground, with their head right next to my fresh new sneakers. So, muthafuckas started calling me Left. I kinda liked that shit, too.

Every morning after a night spent playing with the crackheads, when Moms walked into my room, she saw a sight that made her mad. I was fast asleep. Towering over my bed one day, she said, "What the *fuck*? Are you ever going back to school? What are you going to do with yourself? You're seventeen years old! The school keeps calling me and sending letters. I don't know what to tell them."

I rolled over, groggy from the night before. "Nah. I'm not going back. You can go and sign me out, so they can stop bothering you."

It had been almost twenty days straight that I hadn't been to school, or at least that's what the attendance sheets said. The school had been harassing Moms, trying to find out where I'd been. She didn't know. The reality was that I was pulling down $1,000 a week. Like KRS-One said, *Tell me what the fuck am I supposed to do?*

*

July 8, 2011

Today, I've officially been in jail for a month. 19 more to go. The 4th of July weekend done came & went. The family came to visit me at Oneida. It was a 3 day weekend so I was on the dance floor for 3 days—Sat, Sun & Mon. Gutta, HO & Doe came to see me Saturday. We chopped it up, had some laughs. Then Ish & the kids came to see me Sun & Mon along with my mom. The previous week Ni and Lene came, so I've had the dance floor poppin since I been down. LOL. In case you haven't bidded, the dance floor is what they call the visiting room. I'm like Fred Astaire to these niggas. Ha Ha. I was a lil sad on the 4th 'cause that's the day I usually do my annual BBQ with a lot of my friends & family and light up some fireworks for the kids. They love it. But this year they spent it visiting me in prison and taking a long 3 hour journey back home. I went to my cell that night and thought about how I'm inconveniencing them all and how Brittney is struggling with the whole situation. She hates seeing me like this. She didn't even come back on Mon. At first I was mad but I can't really blame her. I don't even like seeing me like this. I won't even take pictures on the visits 'cause I don't want these memories. I was happy to see her tho. A child will never

*understand a parents love until they have kids of their own,
and I love her with all my heart. The boys are holding up well.
Jordan didn't come either but he's still young and doesn't quit
understand. Lil Rule is just that lil me my lil solider rite by his
mother's side where I told him he needs to be while I'm gone. He's
only 11 but he's starting to grasp the meaning of Being A Man.*

*I would've written sooner but I'm just now getting paper
'cause they packed me up and shipped me out for my court date,
which was one hell of a ride. I've only been in jail a month and
already been to 5 different prisons. It's like I'm on a jail tour or
some shit. The Marshals came and got me from Oneida to take
me to Oneida County Jail. Why they did that I have no fuckin
idea. It was a real shit hole. They told me I'd have to stay there
a few days till they came back and got me to bring me to Jersey
for my court date. I was mad as a motherfucker that they put
me in the dirtiest fuckin cell they could find. So much for being
a superstar. LOL. I swept, moped & scrubbed my cell best I
could and went to sleep. When I awoke to the sound of officers
banging on my door it was like their lips were moving in slow
motion and their words came out slurred when they said "Atkins
were shipping you out." I jumped up, brushed my teeth wit some
shit that was supposed to be toothpaste, took a bird bath at the
sink and hurried the fuck outta there hoping the next stop was
at least a real jail and not no county bullshit. When I got to the
front it was the same marshals that dropped me off. They were
fans and did me a favor by coming back so soon, knowing this
jail was a rat hole. These guys were like angels sent to take me to
hell. It would be a long 4-hour drive but at least they were kind
enough to feed me. We had Dunkin Donuts for breakfast and*

McDonald's for lunch as we drove rite past the exit to my house on Rt 17. I hope I get the chance to return the favor one day. Steaks on me fellas. You never know, as life works in mysterious ways, which brings me to my new found hell, Essex County Correctional Facility "The Green Monster."

*

FIVE

—

Hollering

ELEVENTH GRADE SEEMED LIKE THE RIGHT TIME. THE DAY THAT I dropped out of school was a day when I was actually on my way to school. When I came downstairs that morning, I noticed several cars lined up with white men in the driver's seat on the block. They saw me, a black guy, on the way to school and they assumed that I had drugs. I saw them, white men in the hood at eight a.m., and I knew what they wanted. When I approached the first car, they said they were looking for red tops. This was actually a green top neighborhood and I wasn't supposed to be selling on that block. Apparently my "work" was good so they came back for more. I couldn't turn down an opportunity to make money. I was the only one who had any reds, but they were upstairs, in the crib, in my room, hidden in the corner of my closet, underneath my sneakers in a sock. I told them to wait, I'd go get them. I was going to be late to school again.

There was no one hustling in the mornings. My man Gee was a lieutenant on the block. Me and Gee went way back, to when Gee started a wrestling ring when we were in elementary school. Tyray and me would imitate the moves we saw on WWF. Gee worked it out with the bosses of the block so that I could do the morning shift and keep the sneak hustlers off the block.

Other hustlers on the block were stepping to Gee asking, "Who's this l'il nigga?"

Gee handled it for me. "No one is working in the morning, anyway. And, he has *heat*, so he can take care of business if he needs to."

I got the job.

On the warm mornings, I hustled in my underwear, boxer shorts and a T-shirt. I cut out the backs of my sneakers and turned them into slippers. Slipper sneakers, I called them. It was a comfortable uniform that I wore every day. I was running up and down the stairs so many times, I had to be comfortable.

The morning shift became popular and suddenly there were a few of us out there, slinging in the morning. It was me, Gizmo, Snails and Pie-Faced Mel, mostly.

When the morning hustle was on, school was permanently off. That's how the streets won over school.

Aisha said my eyes were starting to look a little crazy when I mixed weed, alcohol and mescaline together. In those days, I didn't care. I couldn't really feel a thing. I was numb. I kept my mind strictly on money and music so I didn't have to feel the hole that was growing inside of me. None of us had fathers, so we were all doing the same shit to deal with it. I just wanted to make money and not have to care about anything else. I was *bugging*. The block had become my home.

Moms knew everything but didn't say anything. Moms was sniffing out the shift in me. She also noticed all of the money that I was leaving around. She would glimpse the stack of bills on the table when I was in the shower, but she wouldn't mention it. Moms was noticing other strange things like opening up our mailbox and finding small little baggies filled with crack rocks. When she asked me about it, of course I blew up in denial.

"Ma, it's not mine! I told them niggas to stop using our mailbox for that shit!" Moms knew whose shit it really was, but it was just too much for her to do and undo. All of her friends' sons were hustling, too.

Life had hit me and I had to hit back, just like Moms told me to.

DRUG DEALING WAS *REAL SHIT,* like Mic Geronimo said. We called the drugs our "work." In the early days, the work was packaged in multicolored capsules that we got from the Chinese man. The Chinese man was in the lucrative business of selling the colorful caps. Each primary-colored cap represented the block and the dealer in charge. The safest place for hustlers to keep their "work" was in our mouths. When we were hustling sometimes we'd have to run from cops or other hustlers who thought you'd taken their customer.

A hustler's challenges were many but the addicts lined up religiously. They were like an army of ants; sadly creeping towards five minutes more of joy while flushing their life down the toilet.

The crack high was like no other, that's what the fiends said. It was a burst of quick excitement that they called euphoria. It was a feeling that was apparently worth five or ten dollars out of every paycheck, twenty dollars out of their grocery money, then the fifty dollars out of their water bill, and then a hundred out of their rent money . . . until it was all gone to my homies and me.

I had started to work the fifteen- and twenty-floor highrises, all uniformly encased in weathered red bricks, all smothering the breath of Black people whose only need was a little more personal space. Whether they were co-ops or projects, the buildings were all the same to me.

My homies and me were all hustling within the same area around 205th and Hollis Avenue—the 2/5th we called it. I was on 1-9-1 Woodhull, which for me was the smarter hustle. We were selling red "31 Illusion Capsules." The vials made the rocks look bigger, which is why they were called *illusion* capsules. They were selling on 205 for five dollars, which was a big vial for a low price. Ten blocks away the money was more lucrative. On 1-9-1 the same thing was going for twenty dollars.

I left the 2/5th because although the money was better, the Jamaicans worked 99th Avenue and our corner was becoming a free for all. The way it worked was we would all wait for the cars to pull up and then pure chaos would ensue. We would run to the cars and swarm around them like bees. We would hiss like snakes, *"My shit, my shit, my shit . . ."* The first one of us to get our vials into the car window would get the sale. That was a crazy way to hustle.

One night, I returned to 99th Avenue and started a war with the Jamaicans that almost got me killed. The war went on for weeks.

IT ALL STARTED because the cops were getting called to the block on the regular, and they seemed to be always looking for my crew. We knew that the Jamaicans were calling them to take attention off of their scandalous shit.

That night, it was unusually quiet on the block. It was like a ghost town. I saw one straggler car roll up to the spot. I ran over to the customer's car. A Jamaican saw him too and just as I was shoving my vial through the window, the Jamaican was trying to push his in at the same time. The customer took my vial, handed me the cash and I thought it was over. But it wasn't.

The Jamaican got me hemmed up as he raged, "This bombo claat bwoy gwan mek me blow off 'im hed, ya no maan." He held his machete over my head. His big eyes widened. All I had was a boom box that I threw at him to get him the fuck off of me.

Out of the darkness came Barrington and Lenox, two of the most notorious Jamaican guys in the crew. One put a Mac-10 to my stomach and the other a gun to my head. I remember not feeling anything but the unforgiving weight of the metal gun against my sweating temple. I wasn't afraid. I was just there, in this life that I chose. Bruthas were getting killed around me, every day. Today was just my day.

"You know bwoy you don't wuk over here anymore. Move from 'round here. We own dis here spot. Ya betta run pun the tren track and don stop."

Junior's heavy Jamaican patois accent roared in my ear. I was beyond the point of being scared.

I knew they were going to shoot me in the back of my head, which is a punk way to murder a homie, if I must say so myself.

Shit was hectic and I started making my plans as I started to run through a tunnel in the neighborhood to the safe side. My brain was running faster than my feet. My heart was pumping and my eyes were twitching with sheer terror. I figured if I ran to the end of the tunnel and got up the stairs I would come out on the other side of 1-9-1. If I could get up on the tracks they wouldn't be able to catch me.

POP! POP! POP! I heard the bullets flying above and around me, hitting walls and parked trains. *They were giving me a break.* If they hadn't shot me when their gun was at my temple, those boys weren't going to take me out at all. I was relieved but my feet kept running, just in case. I ran like someone running away from the past. I ran like someone searching for what was missing.

The beef continued for a couple more weeks. It seemed that every day *more* shit popped off. There were several more shoot-outs and conflicts. A few people got shot. Flakes got killed. There was always shit going on in the hood, just like when my man Gee was paralyzed.

Then, after a couple of weeks and too many casualties, the 99th Avenue beef just quieted down on its own.

WITH BAD, THERE'S always some good. The streets in Queens were popping. I would see all the big-time rappers. I remember LL Cool J just riding through in his BMW. In fact, he dated a relative of Aisha's at some point. I recall Run DMC in 192 Park. They were freestyling "Here We Go," and it seemed like three weeks later it was a hit record, playing on the radio. I would see Onyx in the neighborhood. Seeing these dudes around made me feel like I could make it. I would even freestyle in the 192 Park and folks would cheer me on. Deep down the cheers made me feel I could make it.

I WAS AFRAID OF AISHA loving me too much. I was a young Black man in the game who had already been arrested for drugs and guns. It was a life that I had chosen and it would be complicated to get out of, even if I tried. You see, thugs don't care if you have made a decision to better your life. They still see you as the thug you were and always will be.

"I should love you more than you love me, because you could lose me," I said to Aisha one time.

"Don't say that, Jeffrey! We all have something to live for now. We have each other."

"I know. I know. I want to live, but brothas are out there

losing their lives . . . there's just no guarantees in these streets."

"Don't say that again! You sound crazy, Jeffrey. I'm not going to let you die. The men who are dying are dying because they have nothing to live for. You have me."

THE POLICE KNEW US. And we knew them well. We had all figured how to coexist in the hood. Our same officers were assigned to patrol our block every day. We had nicknames for them like Tango and Cash and Robo Cop. The lines between reality and cop dramas were blurred. We named our cops after the characters from the movies that entertained us after school and on the rare nights we stayed home. We watched the shows late at night through bloodshot eyes. During the days, on the block, we'd become actors, laughing and jeering at cops and running from ourselves. To each other we called the cops by their nicknames and I could hear the cops calling me "Left" from behind.

In the winter, I would dress for the weather while sitting on my black milk crate waiting for the corner phone to ring. I was bundled up in a wool cap, a lined Carhartt jacket and my 40 Below Timberland boots. We each had a cell phone and a pager but we also gave out the corner phone number to friends and family as if it were our private line. It made sense to us because the corner was where we were when we weren't at home.

THE SKILLED HUSTLERS were invisible and visible at the same time. We wanted to be invisible to the cops, but visible to our customers. I wanted the other hustlers to know I had heat, so that they would have respect, but I didn't want the cops to know, so I had to hide it. As I stood on that corner, I sometimes had rhymes rolling around in my head.

Listen up, I got a story to tell
On the streets we got guns and drugs for sale
And you hoes know the game that we play is real
Keep your mind on the money and your weapons concealed. . . .

Holding the work on our person made us targets, which made guns a necessity. Hiding them on top of the tires of the car parked in front of us was the best way to keep the heat off of us but give us quick access in case something jumped off.

Not everyone had one. It just depended on your job. After the Jamaican war, I started to carry mine all the time, just to be safe. Carrying a gun created a new set of worries. It was power and fear all in the same breath. I feared that I would have to pull the trigger. I never feared being shot myself. That's just not how you think when you have a gun. You're always the shooter, at least that's what you tell yourself.

The lookouts made sure that there were no cops around. They would dip and dive between buildings—hiding out and surveying the land. They knew the cops and the cops knew them.

The lieutenants were the ones that stirred the sales and gave out the work to the hustlers. Lieutenants made sure the money was coming in right. The workers (hustlers) were the ones that sold the crack to the fiends. I've always been a worker. That suited me because I'm a people person. I liked working with the people and getting my loot as a direct result of the work that I provided.

The gunners made sure that no one would stick up the block. The chefs were cooking up the crack, sometimes in their own kitchens. That shit seemed too bold for me, preparing that shit in Moms' kitchen. My man O's "work" was truly homemade.

My income depended on the generosity of my bosses. On some blocks we was getting 80/20 splits, on others it was 70/30. Some muthafuckas were selling so much crack they were giving 90/10 splits. If you could hustle and move twenty packs a day with a 90/10 split you were pulling in $200 day. That was *$1,000 a week.*

Then, the vials became a problem. They got too bulky so we started using tiny baggies to hold more drugs in our mouths. One nice-sized rock could fit into each baggie. Of course, the size of the rocks was not an exact science. The chefs would try their best to make sure that the size of the rocks was uniform. But sometimes, it didn't work that way. And sometimes the fiends would complain as we shivered on the cold-ass corner.

"This one seems a little small," a crackhead named Boo would always say, as if he was picking out a piece of chicken at a buffet. He would gaze at me with wild, sunken eyes, and missing teeth, and his quivering lips would whine, *"Please, man, can I get a bigger one?"*

That shit would make me so heated. Being choosy when you're a drug fiend didn't make sense to me. I hated the fiends because they reminded me of my father and the life I was living because he split. I would look Boo right in the eye and say, "Get the fuck outta here."

Shit.

SOMETIMES WHEN THERE WAS A LULL in traffic, I'd stand back and survey the scene that I was starring in. I would look at my customers. There were so many that I recognized from my life around the way. The faces were from the streets, school and my building. There were too many older faces that I knew because I once went to school with their kids, who had also become my customers.

It was fucked-up to see what people were going through. They all were letting their jobs, their homes, their children and their mates slip through their fingers without a second thought. All because of drugs. I ain't gonna lie, that shit was depressing as fuck.

We had a saying on the block, *"If they ain't buying it from me, they buying it from somebody else. May as well be me."* This motto clouded my brain, stopping clarity from getting in. The motto was all I could hear through my weed-highs and selfish needs. In those days, I didn't give a fuck about anything or anybody. With loot, I could take Aisha to Red Lobster and get all of the gold fronts, three-finger rings and Carhartt jackets that I wanted. I definitely could have used some guidance in my life at that point.

It was a hard thing watching how crack destroys people, but girls particularly. There were too many Tanishas, Kims, and Tonyas to name. It seemed like only a couple of weeks would go by and they had all sunken into shriveled fragments of their former selves. Tanisha was on the fat side in October. By Thanksgiving, she was slack-jawed and skinny. Her juicy ass was all gone and all that was left was flat and bones. Kim used to have a beautiful smile in the summer, but when the kids were back in school in September, her front teeth were shit brown and rotting out of her mouth. Her lips had formed an ashy rim around them and she was constantly licking them, looking for the saliva in her mouth that was no longer being produced. Tonya's hair used to be so pretty and long. Now it stands all over her head, unkempt and unclean. These women had been reduced to fiends. They were no longer human. They were stick-figure sketches drawn in permanent ink, dangling in reality, never to be erased.

We were all getting high off one substance or another to numb us from our reality, the reality of struggle.

BESIDES, I WAS ON TO bigger and better things. Another motto we had was *work less and make more money,* so I started selling harder drugs, heroin. We sold it out of apartments and not on the streets because the junkies needed to shoot up as soon as they got it. That's why heroin was such a great hustle. We knew for sure that the dope fiends would be back because if they didn't come back, they'd get *physically* sick.

Business was so good that I started selling heroin in Schenectady with Chuck and my friend P. We called ourselves "the Four Horsemen," even though there were only three of us. That shit made us laugh our asses off. We were traveling back and forth for weeks at a time to sell heroin. We had customers, but to cut travel costs, we lived with one of our customers where we would stay for three weeks at a time. Chuck had a car and as we drove the three hours each way, Chuck and P would let me freestyle for them. They let me do my thing all the way up there and back. We never listened to the radio, it was strictly time for me to work on my shit. That's the way it was when I was with my real homies. They encouraged me. They knew that if I worked hard enough I could blow up and not have to hustle.

Chuck introduced us to Tameka and the Four Horsemen became her lifeline. We used to trade her drugs in exchange for a place to stay when we came to sell. Tameka was a young single Black mother. I could tell that Tameka once had a pretty face. Now her small face drooped and sagged like her life. Tameka lived with her seven-year-old son, Marcus, who had no dad and reminded me of myself.

Every time we went to Schenectady, I felt like I was walking into my past. Although Moms never had a bunch of thugs staying in our house or giving me drug money as allowance, it was the empty spaces in the house that reminded me of my own. Everywhere I walked, something seemed to be missing and it was called a father. Whatever I said to Marcus made him smile from ear to ear. Even when I told his l'il ass to go to bed. Whatever attention I gave Marcus was like candy. In those small moments with Marcus, I was filling his holes with what I was missing.

Sitting there in Schenectady, I saw how sad and true it is that so many of us experience tough upbringings. We come from broken homes, broken hearts and broken spirits. We come from homes that suffer from not enough money, not enough food and too many ways to escape. That's where the mischievous criminal mentality is born. It is kids, the unwanted and the have-nots who take it on.

P, Chuck and I would make ourselves at home, spreading out all over her place, bagging up drugs, drinking 40s, rolling joints and sleeping through the days when we weren't working. We thought we were making money while providing a male role model for Marcus. It was obvious that Tameka could barely take care of him. We would buy him clothes, buy all of his meals from McDonald's and give him some spending money when we could spare it. We told him to save it and not to spend it. Whenever I handed him another dollar, I'd say, "Stay in school. Get your education, l'il man." While we stayed with Tameka, we also serviced the rest of the neighborhood.

Whenever I had some downtime, I had a notebook in my hand. Marcus thought I was smart. He looked up to me. I was scribbling rhymes. I was still working hard on "Story to Tell." The line just stared back at me from the page:

And just to get to God, I'll go through hell . . . and leave the world with a story to tell.

Then, the rest of the chorus came:

Listen up I got a story to tell
I'm prayin to God, I know I'm goin' to hell

If it's out of my hands, I'll let time prevail,
Listen up I got a story to tell

"What are you writing?" Marcus asked me when he caught me with the pen.

Without looking up, I said, "A rhyme."

"What's that for?" he said, his face all scrunched up.

"You know the rap songs you hear on the radio? I'm writing a song like that. Mine's is gonna be on the radio, too, someday," I said, hoping what I was saying was true.

"What's it about?"

"My life," I said, peering around at his crumbling life.

"What's this?" Marcus asked.

Without looking up, I said. "Put it down, man."

"Look at me!" Marcus said dramatically. When I looked up he was holding one of the guns that P left on the couch. He was posed with the gun pointed at me like he had seen it on TV a million times.

"Marcus, put that down! You could hurt yourself with that, man! That's only for grown-ups. You promise you won't touch it ever again?"

"I promise," he said, pouting, hoping that he hadn't made me mad.

IF YOU GIVE PEOPLE GUNS, they'll use them. It was like the wild, wild west sometimes in the hood. Often for no reason, bruthas just wanted to shoot up places. Shit would pop off instantly and there would be a shootout on the block or in someone's backyard. For those who didn't get shot, it was funny and made lots of great stories that would be told over and over again with new details and a slightly different twist every time. They would be shooting each other over something as petty as a game of dice.

I remember the time my homies Champ and LayLay were blazing one night out on the Boulevard. Champ had a nine-millimeter Glock and LayLay had a semiautomatic. They were playing a game of dice and one of them rolled and the die went into the crack in the concrete. No one watching the game could really decide what it said.

"It's a six, nigga!" Champ argued. "You owe me."

"Nigga that's a two! "

They went back and forth about what the dice said and then Champ just started blazing. Everyone scurried, running for their lives. People were jumping into garbage dumpsters, hiding behind doorways and ducking down behind mail-boxes as soon as they started shooting at each other. After the police were called and the sirens finally quieted, everyone on the block just went back to what they were doing. No one was hurt that time.

You could be at a house party with all the honeys looking sweet and bruthas dressed tight and some muthafucka would pop his trunk and suddenly people were scurrying like roaches, running and jumping over fences to get the fuck out of the yard.

Another time we were at a house party and someone tried to holla at one of the chicks. She told him that she had a man. Apparently because he wasn't there, this dude thought he could holla at her anyway. The girl wasn't checking for no one else. After a while, he got mad and left the party with his boys and after an hour they came back to shoot up the place.

When I realized that shots were ringing out, we all dropped our drinks and I yelled *"Shiiit!"* as Devin and I ran out the back door and over the gate. Chuck was right behind me. At least, I thought he was. When I looked again, he and Devin were gone. The alley seemed to swallow them up. They had ducked into a storefront and locked the door. When I caught a glimpse of them, I went back but they had locked me out. All that was out there to help me survive was another fence that could possibly get me out of that shit. I jumped over and there was a gray-and-white pit bull looking at me like dinner.

As sweat poured down my face. I slowly slumped down off the fence, avoiding eye contact with the pit. I moved slowly. I moved slowly, carefully and quietly. The pit watched me. I slowly walked across the yard in front of him and respectfully excused myself. That shit was *close*.

—

SIX

Screaming

ANYTHING CAN HAPPEN. BLACK SURPRISED ME WHEN HE TOLD me that he had been going to the studio and playing around with some rhymes. He always said he wasn't serious about rapping even though I knew he had skills. He came to me with a cassette tape that he'd made with his man DJ Irv, and Irv was working with named Mic Geronimo. They were just playing around, freestyling and shit. I listened to these mix-tape joints and they were not bad at all. Black's skills were definitely there.

"Yo, I want to go to the studio with you next time. Put me on."

Black said, "Bet. I told you I wanted to introduce you to Irv, anyway."

"I thought you were just a street nigga who happens to rap. This shit here is dope."

"I'm just playing around. Next time, I'll put you on."

"I'm ready for that shit. Let's make it happen."

DJ IRV MET MIC GERONIMO at a high school talent show. It seems like they met and all of a sudden, Geronimo had a record out, called "Shit's Real." TVT records had made a low-budget grainy video, but it was a *video*, nonetheless. Mic Geronimo was crazy *dope* on the mic, but I was confident that my skills could definitely hang with his. Black thought he was taking me to the studio like a fan or some shit, he didn't know I was playing to win.

The wicked aroma of weed is the cologne of hip-hop and it caught us as soon as we walked into the building.

I was ready to do this.

The recording studio was actually an apartment that Irv's friend owned. It was a small space but it had a mixing board, a makeshift microphone and some do-it-yourself soundproofing. The booth where Mic was recording was tiny but it got the job done.

The studio was dimly lit with candles. There was an assortment of menus, pizza boxes and ashtrays on the coffee table. My senses were on overload. The smells of the weed and the pop and buzz of the wiring swept over me. I wanted this to be my life.

BLACK HAD BEEN BRAGGING about knowing Irv for a long time. He introduced me, saying, "This is my man, Ja Rule, the MC I was telling y'all about. He's *nice*. You should check him out."

(My friends called me "Ja" based on my initials, short for Jeffrey Atkins. Then one day, when we were at the park, Kamal B. Wise who was part of a group called Total Pack, put the "Rule" on the end. It caught on real fast and stuck.)

When Mic Geronimo came out of the booth, I could see myself standing where he stood. He was just a regular dude with gold fronts and a low-cut fade.

I didn't know what the best approach would be. Should I just start freestyling right there? Should I shake hands or should I just wait until they invited me to do something? I looked over Mic Geronimo's shoulders into the makeshift booth that was once a closet. My eye stayed on the microphone. DJ Irv was ready to be entertained. He looked at me and gestured towards the booth with his chin.

"Enter at your own risk," he said with a sly grin.

I had no fear.

I walked into the booth and Irv gave me a beat. I asked him to slow it down slightly to match the song that I'd been working on.

Listen up I got a story to tell
I'm prayin to God, know I'm goin to hell
If it's out of my hands, I'll let time prevail, huh
Listen up I got a story to tell
Son in B'more, we scored more, than ever before
Copped the two-door, six-double-oh off a raw
Show no love for loss since big eight be that lucky
Number, we slammed eight of those in Kentucky
Kept the currency comin, mo', diamonds

New clothes LA hoes that'll ride us pronto
Once you, lived in luxury, you can't leave it
Find yourself, turnin' broke bitches into divas
Can you believe this?
And just to get to God, I'll go through hell
And leave the world with a story to tell, heh
Listen up I got a story to tell
On the streets we got guns and drugs for sale
And you hoes know the game that we play is real
Keep your mind on the money and your weapons concealed, huh

Listen up I got a story to tell
I'm prayin to God, know I'm goin to hell
If it's out of my hands, I'll let time prevail
Listen up I got a story to tell

DJ Irv's head was bobbing. He was impressed with my skills. He liked my energy and the fact that I didn't want to come out of the booth. Mic Geronimo was feeling me, too. When I finished "Story to Tell," I walked out of the booth and DJ Irv rushed me with the most important question, "You freestyle, too?"

"No doubt," I said.

I spit something off the top of my head.

I handled my business.

"I like your confidence, man," he said, looking me straight in the eye.

Irv turned to Black and said, "Y'all should become a group. Ja Rule, O and you too, Black. Think about it. I think it could work."

Mic Geronimo gave me a pound. "That's what's up."

When we got downstairs, Black handed me a joint that he had in his pocket. He lit it and took the first drag. "Let's make this shit happen."

I took the joint and looked at it long and hard. "Okay," I said. Smoke burst out of my mouth as I said, "It's about time."

BLACK CALLED IRV and told him that we were going to start the group, as he recommended.

"If you put it together, I'll do the rest. I have a lot of shit about to jump off. I can make it happen," Irv assured Black.

When Black got off the phone, he looked at us and said, "What shall we call ourselves?"

We went to the source, which was our favorite movie, *New Jack City*. We had been watching it weekly since 1991 when it first came out. It was about an infamous drug dealer named Nino Brown. Nino Brown changed my life. Nino was calm, cool, collected and driven. He was the shit. He had money, women, guns and most importantly, he had *power*.

Everyone we knew in the hood was going through hard times, but on-screen, all the obstacles that were in our way seemed to disappear. At the time, *New Jack City* was the only movie that represented the East Coast. Most of the movies that were out, at that time, were West Coast–centered. Movies like *Boyz N the Hood*, *Menace II Society* and *Colors*. Being from the East Coast, I wanted to know why they were killing each other over generational beefs? Out there, it is like: "My father and uncle died in this, so I guess I must represent by defending the family." This is the philosophy that was portrayed in West Coast movies. Our thing, on the East Coast, was all about getting money. It was nothing personal. It was just business for us. What the movie *New Jack City* represented was success in a way that seemed attainable. At that time, we believed that the only way out of the hood was to play basketball or some other sport, rapping and drugs. Those were our options.

Whenever we would dive into that large screen of the movies, it was as if we had been magically transported off the block, leaving all the powerlessness that came with the hood. The lines were blurred between what we saw in our movie heroes and who we were. We wanted badly for it to be one and the same.

In the movie, Nino Brown ran a whole building called The Carter in Harlem. It was like a small corporation. Nino's crew was called the Cash Money Brothers and so naturally, Black, O and I named our group the Cash Money *Click*.

"That's it!" Black said while we were watching *New Jack City* for the one hundredth time.

"Word," said O.

"I'm feeling it. That shit is tight," I agreed.

We started working on a rhyme called "Get tha Fortune," because for us, it wasn't about the fame, it was always about getting the paper.

The three of us spent many nights at Dyna Dog studio where I had just met Mic Geronimo. Irv had arranged some free studio time for us to get our joint ready. The studio was so hood that we used a stocking over a hanger to make a spit foam in front of the microphone. When we were in the studio, we would drink whole bottles of Rémy Martin and smoke bags of weed. I had a growing tolerance for drugs and alcohol, or a deeper need to escape, and I didn't care which one it was.

In the studio, we'd get so high that we could barely see. I must admit that I loved the feeling of being high. It gave me something that nothing else could, except for sex. I believed that being high pushed my creativity. The Rick James song "Mary Jane," which came out two years after I was born, was *still* a legendary anthem to weed.

The music had always been at full volume ever since the days that O and I were the nomads, a couple of years before. We recorded in my man C-Style's basement studio. I always remember how my man's basement would shake and rattle at the deafening beats that were busting out of the speakers.

Although there were forty-ounce bottles all over the floor and ashes, cigarettes and remnants of joints buried in the upholstered sofa that was spilling its foam guts, I was at home down there, even then. I was more at home there than on the block, running up and down the stairs or giving crack to fiends. The studio has always been the only place that I could feel blood running through my veins. Aisha complained that I was never home, but I was keeping the promise that I had made to her and to myself.

TVT RECORDS HAD A TASTE OF SUCCESS with Mic Geronimo in 1994. "Shit's Real" was instantly an underground hit. It made it to number twenty-three on the *Billboard* hip-hop charts. Steve Gottlieb of TVT understood that underground rap was a market unto itself and was looking for the next big thing to give his small indie label some more relevance to the ever-growing hip-hop phenomenon.

Irv promised he would share our tape with Steve as soon as it was finished.

When Irv told us that Steve was interested in signing us, without a second thought, we went straight downtown to meet him. We had big dreams and dollar signs in our eyes. We didn't know anything about how the music business worked. All we knew was that Mic Geronimo had a deal and a video and soon we would too.

Steve Gottlieb was a short white dude with a long black ponytail. He looked more like a hippie than someone who knew anything about hip-hop. He walked around the office in his bare feet. When Irv took us down to the Village, where the TVT office was located, we couldn't help but notice how stark and corporate it was. Lots of white walls, desks and computers. There was no music playing, only the sound of lawyers and accountants making spreadsheets and crunching numbers. The most obvious problems were the blinding fluorescent lights and the fact that the air was clear. There was no one smoking weed, except for one man in the conference room, Gil Scott-Heron. At the time, I didn't know him by face, but I knew his music and the Last Poets. Gil was always in the conference room smoking and we were glad to join him. We would talk as often as we could. Since we were young, Gil schooled us on the business. He talked to us about his ups and downs in the business. I value the time we spent with him and I will never forget it.

We were all sitting in his office around his little round desk. "I like your sound. And, I like your name," Steve said with a silly white-boy grin, his bare feet propped up on the desk, wiggling his toes.

Although he never said it, I realized that Steve liked the idea that we were hustlers, which would give TVT the street credibility they wanted.

Everyone at TVT sat on the same floor so the office was kind of boring. There was no creative vibe in there at all. The A&R guys were sitting right next to the lawyers. Everything was white in the office, especially Steve and his staff. Steve was a different kind of dude. He was one of those white hippie kids who looked like a hippie but his looks were deceiving because he went to Yale undergrad and Harvard Law School. All I knew about him was that he was going to give us money and a video. The rest didn't matter.

"Get the Fortune, muthafuck the fame," was the first line of the rhyme that we had been working on. My verse started:

Don't risk it, Ja Rule's known for makin fat shit
Fully-loaded clip, usin' wax for targets
Rattattat, rewind the DAT, Black
I got your mind wide open and your wig pushed back

GOTTI WAS PROUD when he presented us with a stack of small-print contracts and a $10,000 check to be split evenly between the three of us. All of us were high as fuck as we posed with Steve and Irv for our signing photograph. The photo would go under a similar picture with Irv and Mic Geronimo. Mic and Cash Money Click would be the only rap artists at TVT. There was a lot of history at TVT. That's where I first met Treach and Trent Reznor from Nine Inch Nails. Trent was trying to get off TVT. He was telling us how much of a thief Steve was.

Steve missed out on signing many acts. TVT could have been Def Jam. Many rappers approached TVT before going to Def Jam, which was becoming an institution. TVT was independent and an ideal place for a startup rather than going to Warner or Universal to get your stuff placed. Steve passed on Dr. Dre's *The Chronic*. He passed on Snoop, The Lady of Rage, Jay-Z and DMX. All of that was brought to his desk before it went anywhere else. He eventually went on to lose me and Nine Inch Nails. Steve didn't get it. He wasn't in tune with the culture.

Black, O and me all laughed our asses off at the TVT check when we left the meeting. That $3,300 each was *no* fortune to us. We were already pulling down decent money on the streets. The three of us finally decided what would make the most sense would be for us to buy $10,000 worth of crack and flip it. Then, we would all make some *real* paper.

We would release our first single with "4 My Click" as the A-side and "Get tha Fortune" as our B-side. We would get two videos out of the deal, not just one. We didn't have money to shoot the video the way we wanted to for "Get tha Fortune." They only gave us $10,000 to sign, so it can be imagined what the budget was to shoot the video. The budget was low, low, low. We were on a shoestring budget, but we had plans to get around that.

Gotti was friends with Hype Williams. He had done videos with Jodeci, Mary, and Busta. Hype was the man. We were all from Queens. Gotti asked Hype for a favor.

"We got this new group. We need to do two videos because we want to do a video for the B-side, too."

Hype said he'd make it happen. He was shooting a video for Mary J. Blige, "Be Happy." This was a big-budget video. Hype "borrowed" some of the film so we could have 35mm film to shoot with, instead of the low-budget 16mm film. We made it happen. We shot "Get tha fortune." Thanks Mary! This is how you grind. You have to do whatever you have to do to make it happen.

One of our videos would be shot in a gritty staircase in Queens on Hollis Avenue and the other one would be filmed in a shop that was owned by our man Preme. We didn't have lighting. I remember we had to bring a lamp from my apartment. People around the way were happy to see us shooting a video on their block, *hundreds* of people came out to cheer us on and to get on camera whenever they could.

I couldn't wait to tell Aisha that we had a record deal.

I HADN'T SPENT QUALITY time with Aisha in a while so I planned a special night. I was going to have Aisha over to hang with me at the crib to celebrate the record deal.

My Moms rarely cooked, so I couldn't offer her a home-cooked meal, so I would be the cook that night. I went to the C-Town supermarket and bought a pack of cube steaks, a box of Velveeta macaroni and cheese and a few packs of Kool-Aid.

Aisha said it all tasted good. I even made gravy with onion soup and water. We ate a lot and talked a lot. It felt nice being with her in private. After dinner, Aisha and I went to my room. I couldn't wait to tell her about the record deal. We were lying on my bed and I was just about to tell her my exciting news. But Aisha had something to tell me, too. I let her go first.

"Guess what?" Aisha said with a tentative voice.

"What?" I said.

"I'm pregnant, Jeffrey."

I couldn't believe my ears. We both thought that we were doing the right thing and that it could never happen to us. I was happy but dazed. Although it wasn't good timing, it was perfect timing in some ways. I would be able to take care of us financially, because I now had a record deal. I was on my way. I *wasn't* ready to be nobody's father. I was ready to be a star.

"*Word?* You sure?" I finally said.

"Yeah, I'm sure." Aisha said softly as she put her head down, afraid to see the look on my face.

We had used condoms for the first straight year. And then we don't know what happened. I think I was the one who suggested that we use the "withdrawal method." I'd heard from someone that it worked. Or maybe, I'd heard that it didn't work.

This news from Aisha was the wake-up call I needed. Having a baby would mean that I needed more money and that I *had* to get this rap thing in motion.

"Wow, girl, that's big news, Aisha. How do you feel?" I hoped my face was pleasant, if not neutral.

"I'm not scared . . . maybe a little. Jeffrey, I just don't want to be another statistic. I want to have all my kids with the same man."

Aisha was afraid, I could tell. She was trying to be strong, although I could see her eyes watering. This was that moment in the hood that all chicks fear, the moment when the guy who got her pregnant says, "I'm out." Or, they simply *be* out.

I wasn't going to do that to Aisha. I loved her, even though I was only eighteen. I lightened up the mood for her, like I always did. "Okay. Then have all of your kids with me. Look, we have one out of the way already!" I said, wanting to comfort her and wanting to believe for myself that what I was saying was possible. I was only eighteen years old—nine months from then, where would I be?

"I love you, Jeffrey," she said, pulling me closer to her.

"I love you too, baby girl," I said as my mind wandered to the tour that I hoped I'd be on with Mic Geronimo someday.

I was excited about the baby, but I knew that would mean I would need to make even more money. I wanted the money to come from rhyming and not hustling. If that wasn't the case, it would be true, Aisha would lose me.

"JEFFREY, DO YOU REMEMBER when I told you that I wasn't scared? I lied. Reality hits me every time I see how big my belly is getting.

"Oh my God," she whined, "I'm going to have to take care of this baby all by myself, since you'll be on the road." She rolled her eyes and turned her back as she buried her face into the pillow.

There were a lot of nights like that when we were together but didn't have much to say. Everything that was happening was too heavy to talk about. We just had to let that shit simmer. Talking too much wasn't going to help. The baby talk was starting to scare me, too. I didn't know what to say to her. Was she expecting me to say that I would be there to help with the baby? I couldn't speak too soon. I didn't want to make any promises that I couldn't keep. Shit was popping off for my music. They were planning a tour that I would be on. I would always love the baby and Aisha, forever, but I may not be there to change diapers and shit. I would be out on the road, on stage, signing autographs—where I belonged. I would be being the man that I said I'd be.

I'm a godsend, the fallen angel and I do sin
Far from perfection but still considered a gem
Thank you lord for givin' me wind beneath my wings
When the miracle spittin there shall be no witnesses to da pain
And my ignorance, I charge to da game
So many love and slain by bullets wit dead aim
I weathered the change

I read over the verse one more time. With my verse staring back off the page at me, I wondered why I wrote the word "godsend." Was I a godsend to anyone? Certainly not my father. Was I a godsend to Moms or had I done nothing but give her problems?

For Aisha, I was a godsend, maybe. She did say to me that I

was the most stability she had ever had. She was for me, too. It was in the back of my tattered notebook that was running out of pages. It would soon be time for a new one or to retire those notebooks altogether. The verse was okay, but I wasn't feeling it all the way just yet.

I did have a strange feeling that there was something with me, looking over me. Maybe God didn't forget us, after all. Maybe it was Kristen. I could feel it. Kristen's spirit was giving me wind beneath my wings. I smoked a little more trying to figure it out. A title for this joint finally came to me. "We Here Now." I didn't want to write it down, just yet. I wasn't fully ready to commit to anything.

IN ALL OF THE EXCITEMENT of having a video and a pocketful of drugs to sell, in the blink of an eye, Black got caught out there, and because he had some drug-related priors, he was arrested and ended up doing time.

The dream was dead before it started. The Cash Money Click project was on hold.

From Steve Gottlieb's perspective, five years was a long time for a label to stick to a commitment to a trio with one-third of its members in a cell. He said, "I can't make videos with just the two of you."

DJ Irv was finally getting some recognition as Mic Geronimo's producer. Suddenly, his presence grew and being known as simply DJ Irv was not enough. Jay-Z gave him the nickname Gotti after John Gotti of the infamous Gambino mafia crime family in Brooklyn. Jay-Z was always on that gangster shit.

Gotti liked the name because it symbolized a "Boss" and that is who he wanted to be in the rap game. DJ Irv became Irv Gotti.

In the meantime, Gotti had already started scheming and planning a solo project for me, despite the entanglement with TVT. Steve Gottlieb, who was once our savior, quickly turned into an enemy. Our frustration with the situation was so bad that I started drinking and smoking more than ever. The realization that I would be stuck a hustler for the rest of my life came into full view. There was seemingly nowhere I could go, musically. I had *gotten* a record deal but couldn't record.

I thought about running up in Steve Gottlieb's office with some guns, which would have been easy to pull off. I had heard a rumor that Treach from Naughty by Nature had done this already and got released from the label. Then I realized that *this* situation was not *that* type of a situation. A corporate type like Steve Gottlieb didn't live by the codes of the streets. All he would do is what corporate people do, sue. All that would have happened to me if I ran up in there with guns is the receptionist would push a button under her desk and I would be getting a baton upside my head on my way upstate to be in the same cell with Black.

I REALIZED THEN that I had to do things differently. Different things call for different measures. Although Steve was corporate, he was still a fighter. Steve had the law and a signed contract on his side. I couldn't win and I couldn't get out of the deal. He still held the power no matter how many guns I could get my hands on. I had to face it, my career was dead for the next three to four years.

Even though I had faced the reality, after a while, Gotti and I couldn't sit still anymore. We had a video that was out there and we needed to promote it to spark some more attention despite the situation. We had a strategy that we called "Jack the Box." Back in the day, *The Box* was a cable program that would allow viewers to call in and request the videos that they wanted to see.

Gotti and I would watch the *Box* religiously, and we would time our requests according to whenever Mary J. Blige and Method Man's joint "You're All I Need to Get By" came on. Every time it came on, we would call in to request "Get tha Fortune." Finally, the plan worked. One day, Lyor Cohen, Russell Simmons and Jam Master Jay, God rest the dead, were watching *The Box* and admiring how hot their Method Man and Mary J. Blige video was. It was on *The Box* at least ten times a day. It so happened that "Get tha Fortune" came on right after Mary and Meth.

As I later learned, Jam Master Jay stood up in the meeting and said, "That dude is going to be a fucking star!" He was talking about me. His statement triggered Lyor Cohen and the powers that be at Def Jam to find me by any means necessary. Jam Master Jay had his own studio and although he was working with Def Jam he was also working on his own artists as well. To get their attention was an even bigger honor.

SHIT WAS HAPPENING. I was getting attention from the right people. Jam Master Jay and Def Jam were talking about me and Irv had hooked me up with his friend Jay-Z, who wanted me to be on one of his joints, "Can I Live." He asked me to come meet him in the studio and lay down my verse. When I got there, it was too late. But I learned something from the experience. I learned that I needed to go to the next level.

"Nigga, you late," said Jay-Z as he emerged from the booth. "I think I got it. Sorry about that. I'll put you on another joint soon."

"You did the verse already? Where's your notebook?" I asked.

"Don't have one. It's all in my head," Jay said, proudly.

No way—who the fuck does that? I didn't want to act too surprised, but I was. I couldn't even fathom that he could hold all those rhymes in his head.

I realized that if writing rhymes was what I wanted to do for the rest of my life, I needed to know my shit off the top, like Jay-Z. The paper was just a crutch.

I KNEW JAM MASTER JAY from the neighborhood. And he had a studio on Jamaica Avenue where I could go and meet up with Black Child, who was one of JMJ's artists at the time.

"I love your energy man. How's TVT treating you?" asked Jam Master Jay.

"It's kind of a long story, but I'm not really recording with them right now."

"Word? You should come fuck with me."

Then a chubby kid came in from out the back. I had recognized him from the streets. It was "Boo-Boo," who was now going by the new name, 50 Cent.

"Hey 50, this is Ja Rule. Ja Rule, this is 50 Cent, my new artist."

We had already met. 50 Cent knew who I was, and was a fan.

"Yo like ya new shit. We should do a song together," said 50.

"Yeah, ya'll should put that together," said J.

"Yeah, we could do that," I agreed.

50 was a real quiet dude, not saying much and watching everything I did.

The only one who didn't think that was a good idea was Black Child. Black was Jam Master Jay's top artist. But 50 was starting to become JMJ's favorite. Black felt that if I was going to do a record with anybody it was going to be with him, not 50. So me and 50 never got the chance to do the record. I believe this is where the animosity started.

When I got ready to leave I gave a pound to Jay and his new artist.

Black said when we were outside, "Fuck that nigga." Black didn't really like 50 Cent.

I WAS EXPECTING a baby and Aisha was home alone most nights when I was out partying, or so it seemed. The more Aisha talked about the baby kicking, all I could think about was when I would be on the road and see posters with my face all over the streets.

I realized how much I needed Aisha to keep me on the ground. I wanted to do right by her and the baby, but this was my chance. Shit was so hectic that some days were a blur. As her stomach grew, hip-hop was bigger than ever. My ego was growing and my mind wouldn't stop playing tricks on me. I was taking on the attitude and swagger of the men around me.

This all happened close to my leap year birthday, February 29.

I had started hanging out with more music people and hanging out in clubs trying to meet as many people in the industry as I could. People were showing me some love at the Q Club in Queens and sending over bottles of champagne to acknowledge my birthday. The Cash Money Click single was out and people recognized me. It felt good to finally get some birthday love.

Def Jam had released Mary J. Blige and Method Man and following right behind them they released Foxy Brown and Jay-Z doing another rap/duet. Foxy Brown was a young female rapper who embodied all the things that the hip-hop world was fiending for, a female MC with skills and looks, sex appeal and a gangsta attitude. Foxy Brown was the hottest thing out and her and Jay-Z's joint, "Ain't No Nigga," was ruling the radio. Foxy and Jay-Z were performing that night and I was there to see what my life would have been like if Black hadn't gone to prison. Like I said, the bottles of champagne were being sent to me from all over the club and Foxy Brown noticed. She sent her brother over to me.

"Yo, Rule, my sister wants to meet you."

I didn't recognize him. "Who's your sister?" I asked.

"Foxy Brown," he said, proudly.

"*Word?* Where is she? I would love to meet her."

When I met Foxy, I immediately liked her vibe. She was dope on the mic and she was a cool chick. She had a sex appeal and swag about her that said Brooklyn. I wasn't interested in getting with her, I wanted to pick her brain about the music industry. We exchanged numbers and became cool.

I told Foxy what happened with Black and TVT and that I was stuck in a deal that I couldn't get out of. She listened and told me she would keep me posted. She already knew about "Get tha Fortune." She called me a few days after Lyor had seen the video. She was in the middle of a meeting with Lyor.

"Ja, this is Foxy."

"What's up?" I said, surprised to hear her voice.

"You'll never guess what happened. Lyor is looking for you. They looking to sign some new acts. I told him that I knew you."

"*Word?* I'll take it from here. Good looking out, Foxy."

I called Irv and told him that Def Jam was looking for us. Irv was happy to hear that because he was working with Jay-Z, who also needed a deal. Jay-Z was also a hustler and he had formed his own independent label called Roc-A-Fella. Although he was only an indie, he sold a lot of records on his own. But he was getting antsy, too. He wanted a label deal to take his music to the next level. He and Gotti had a plan.

"Def Jam is looking for some real shit," I told Irv.

"That's all I need to hear. Ya know I got you, Ja."

Def Jam Records is the hip-hop generation's Motown and when I told Aisha that we were actually going to a meeting at Def Jam, she screamed. "See, baby. I knew it would happen for you," she said as she kissed me.

The dream was back on and there was definitely going to be something to live for.

never again will I run down a road so dark
hope to die
cross my heart never again
but these streets keep calling
they keep calling
they keep calling
never again

I looked at the words and thought that I had to get off the streets. I wanted to give my child a chance. A chance that he or she wouldn't have unless I was alive. Dying young really didn't mean shit. It's not a badge to wear on your arm. It's not honor. You're just dead, while the living just go on. Aisha was right, I did have something to live for.

I was going to show her. I'm gonna break the cycle. Muthafuckas don't need more babies out here who don't have a father. Another line came to me and I scribbled it down before I lost it:

Rule spits monotonous, hot as apocalypse
Now you eyein' dis ferocious mic supremist
Whose limits is endless
This nigga here done risen

"I DON'T FEEL WELL," Aisha complained. I was heading to the studio although the baby was due any minute. September 20, 1995, had come and gone and there was still no baby.

"Babe, I'll get with you later tonight after the studio," I promised. "Tell the baby to wait for me."

"Babies don't wait for anyone or anything," Aisha said, angrily.

Later that night, Aisha's cousin, Cheryl, paged me but I was in the studio with O where the reception was poor. After we'd finished laying down some tracks and got the message from Cheryl that Aisha was in labor, we headed directly to the hospital.

When O and I were on the train going to the hospital, I was scared as shit. In a panic, I got off the train and stopped by my Moms' house for support. She told me, "I wasn't there when you made it."

"Just be a man," I heard my Moms' voice say in my head.

I quickly got back on the train. O and I went between the subway cars and smoked a blunt. We were both lost in our own heads. I was trying to accept that after that night, I would never be the same. There's no rulebook on being a father. Most of us had never seen it done. I knew that suddenly I wanted to live to be one hundred. I needed proof of something positive that I had created. I'd destroyed too much shit already. I turned to O and nudged him. He opened his eyes slowly.

"Nigga, you know having this baby will right my wrongs if I do right by the baby and Aisha."

"You have a lot of wrongs to right, nigga." O smiled at me.

"On the serious tip, I mean it. We have to stay alive. Life is all we got. My shit will never be the same once this baby gets here."

"It'll be all good, man. You're just nervous. I wanna stay alive, too. Don't worry. We gotchoo."

When I arrived at the hospital, O and I both reeked of weed. When we checked in at the hospital the doctor came out to meet me and tell me how Aisha was doing. When he smelled the cloud of stink coming out of our clothes, the doctor recoiled, as he stood back and said that he would come get me when Aisha was about to deliver.

When a nurse finally came out to get me a couple hours later, I rushed in to see Aisha. When I got there, Aisha was already holding our daughter in her arms. *What the fuck?* I started to go find the doctor and curse him out because he'd said I'd be able to see the birth. But I didn't make a scene on the day my daughter was born. I was trying to change.

It was September 22, 1995, at seven a.m. that my daughter, Brittney Asja (pronounced "Asia") Atkins, was born. I was nineteen.

I held Brittney in my arms. I wanted to bear her weight, and keep her safe. A quiet feeling of power swept over me like I'd never felt before. Just holding her made me want different things. I wanted *life*. I no longer *hoped* to live, I *needed* to live, for Brittney. I could barely see her through my tears. She was small and precious. I was the only person who could keep her and Aisha safe for the rest of their lives. I was the only one who could be Brittney's father. I was dizzied by the responsibility. I had to sit down.

PART TWO

The Last Temptation

*

July 9, 2011

*My first night here was crazy, inmates screaming, banging and
kicking the doors, calling the male COs bitch ass niggas & faggots,
telling the female COs how they gonna fuck 'em, throwing plates
of food out their cells onto the floor. LOL. WELCOME TO THE
GREEN MONSTER! This type of shit would never happen
upstate. At best, you'd be in the box for a month. At worst,
the infirmary. I even got into it wit these stupid niggas trying
to assassinate my character, talkin about I'm snitching to the
guards and that I'm getting special treatment. I barked on these
niggas and set 'em straight 'cause as a man there's only so much
you can take before you snap. At first I tried to ignore their lil
comments until they started talkin shit like they gonna kick my
door and all this clown shit. But the funny thing is, when I started
screaming on them, lettin them know they got the wrong nigga
they got excited. It was like that's what they wanted, to bring the
hood out of me. That's when I realized that I'm dealing wit kids.
They can't be niggas my age 'cause that would've lead to instant
confrontation, not instant admiration. After I set 'em straight
they wanted to talk & ask me about the industry. I could tell*

they wanted to be my friend but just didn't know how to go about it. So I chatted wit them for a lil bit before letting them know I was tried and ready to lay down. But as I laid, I listened to them talk, telling their life stories of how one was born in a crack house and grew up selling crack to his mother; how another watched his father get murdered right in front of him by some dudes he owed money, as they robbed his house; and how they were now in jail for crimes of their own. One for beating his girlfriend and the other for a murder. One of them is 19 the other just turned 23 yesterday. Both with kids of their own. When will we break the cycle? WILLIE LYNCH LIVES ON . . . DAMN!

When I got here I was happy to see some officers of the same skin color—not that I'm racist or anything, but in this type of situation and where I just came from, you'd be happy to see some of your own, too. Prejudice does still exist, trust me, I've been treated and have seen other people treated like niggers more in 1 month than I have my whole life. I feel like a slave, and even tho I haven't heard anyone say it, actions speak louder than words. As I walk through the door everyone is staring like they can't believe I just walked in cuffed from head to toe. Even tho I don't feel like much of a star that's all they see—the star that has fallen. But as I look in their eyes I still see the love. They still wanna meet me and greet me as if I'm on their own personal stage, except there's no screaming fans, fancy clothes & bright lights. There's only screaming inmates, me in my orange jumpsuit, and little flash lights they shine in my cell at night. It's hard to feel good signing autographs and taking pictures in this predicament but I did it with a smile 'cause I love my fans and never say no,

*no matter what mood I'm in. After the meet & greet they took
me to my cell where I'll be housed till my court date. It's not the
best but it's not the worst either. They gave me some pillows and
an extra mattress so I'll live. This is my 3rd day here and IA
already came and got me to investigate my lil meet & greet. I
basically told them to fuck off and that those are good cops 'cause
they really were nice to me. The last thing I wanna see is good
people get in trouble 'cause they got an autograph or a pic from
me. You wanna investigate something, investigate the crooked
Hip Hop Task Force that got me into this shit in the first place.*

*As I sit in my cell listening to their stories I think about me
and my Dad and how I hated to love him for so many years and
how I vowed to be nothing like him, only to have my mother say,
"You're just like your father." LOL. Which made me curious to
know him. Of course, just as me and my father started to get
closer to one another, he dies. But I have my closure. I learned
a lot about him and him about me in the short time we spent
together. Which makes me think about my kids and how I'm
raising them. I am a great father and I have broken the cycle.
Even though I'm in prison the foundation has already been laid.
I hate being away from them for 20 months, but shit I could have
easily been on tour for that long. I feel compelled, I wanna help
other kids break the cycle.*

*I've been to 5 different prisons and all I see is niggas and
I ain't talking about Black people I'm talking about ignorance.
See the problem wit most people is they don't smell shit until they
step in it and by that time it's all over your shoe and everybody
is tryin to get away from you. Now you have 2 choices, you can*

either wash that shoe or throw it away. A lot of people choose to throw it away, meaning they didn't learn shit. Those that choose to wash that shoe tend to watch their step knowing how hard it was to get 'em clean. I think I'll wash my shoes this time 'cause this shit ain't me.

    R.I.P. William Jeffrey Atkins
    BREAK THE CYCLE!

*

—

SEVEN

Must Be the Music

"DON'T GIRLS GO TO THEIR MOTHER'S WHEN THEY GET PREG-nant and aren't married?" Moms asked in response to my question.

Aisha was living with her Aunt Sarah. Things around the crib had been tense.

"Ma, Aisha don't even live with her moms. Her Aunt Sarah won't take her and the baby. I was thinking that they should come and live with us. Could they?"

Moms was reluctant at first. She didn't even know Aisha that well, which was a sign of the times. Although I love my Moms deeply, we had separate lives.

She thought about it for a long minute and said into the air, "My grandbaby needs a roof over its head. So, I guess we have to do what we have to do."

It was only a two-bedroom apartment. The crib was feeling

crowded with my Aunt Dawn, Uncle Dennis and my man Rich who had all come to stay with us. With Aisha and Brittney moving in, things would have to seriously change.

Moms had that tired look on her face when she said, "Jeff, I need to talk to you about something," She hadn't sounded like that since she signed me out of high school. Moms started, "I know you're trying really hard to do this music thing, but maybe it's not working out. You have responsibilities now. You have a child."

"Moms, trust me. I'm going to make it. Music is what I was *meant* to do. I'm going to do it."

Moms looked at me and shook her head. "We'll all just have to pull together as a family and help with the baby."

Saturday morning, Moms called a meeting for everybody living in the house. We all came to the cramped living room. Me and Aisha and Brittney sat on the couch, Dawn and Dennis were on the love seat. Moms was standing and Rich was already in his usual position, on the floor watching TV.

"Turn off the TV, Richard," she said sternly.

"It's tight in here and it's even tighter now that Brittney and Aisha are living with us. You all can forget your pagers for a while. We should all try to avoid buying new clothes or anything that we don't need. We have to make sure that the rent gets paid, every month and on time." We all listened but no one was willing to give up their pagers. The pagers were what paid the rent.

"Don't think I'm not making sacrifices, too. I've decided to give Kiku and Sabu away," she said sadly.

The room was quiet.

Kiki and Sabu, my Moms' cats, had been her constant companions for many years. They had been through everything with her.

"I worry that they may hurt Brittney. Besides, Brittney is one more mouth to feed and we need the extra money for food and diapers."

I hated sitting there hearing all of this. I didn't want to think that my family was going to be a burden on Moms. I felt restless, I didn't need to hear any more. I had to break out and make some money. I had to head back to the studio.

When the meeting was over, I came up behind Aisha in the kitchen and put my arms around her waist. She usually loved it when I held her like that. "Ish, I need to go back to work and finish the track that Irv and I started."

She whipped around to face me, dropped the dish that she was washing and snapped, "I'm sick of you and the studio. *Brittney* should be your priority!"

"Aisha, I need to do this. I'm not just doing some small shit. I'm making a *record*. I need to do this thing to the highest."

"What's that mean? The highest? We need you here. We need you home!" She grabbed Brittney's rattle off the counter and threw it on the floor. "Do *this* to the highest!" she said with tears in her eyes.

"It's feast or famine now. To put you and Brittney in a better place, I've got to do what I've got to do. Nothing will happen with me sitting here with you and the baby. *Trust me*, Ish. You have to trust me!"

"Jeffrey, I don't want to blindly trust anymore. I want to trust because you're doing what you said you'd do."

Aisha sat on the couch after picking up Brittney's cracked rattle from the floor. As she spoke, she looked down at it. "There've been too many broken promises. I've seen my own father only three or four times in my whole life. My mother struggles so much she can't even take care of us. We've lived all over the place forever, never having a proper home. I can't take any more broken promises. It's sad to say but *you're* the most stability I've ever had. What does that say for my life? You can't desert me now."

I didn't say anything. I just had to show her.

As I walked out the door Aisha screamed, "I *hate* you!"

"No you don't," is all I could say. I was mad at her, too. She should have been saying, "Get out and work . . . go provide for our family!" I knew I wanted to marry Aisha, someday. I knew that she loved me. This was just a really hard time. She loved me, even on that day. Even when I was walking out the door to be with my other true love, hip-hop.

I slammed the door.

HIP-HOP LIVED IN MY EARS twenty-four hours a day. I couldn't turn it off. I wanted to know everything about it so I started to study it like it was a class at John Adams. I wanted to know and hear everything that I could get my hands on. I wanted to understand the art of it, not just memorize all the most popular rhymes like everyone else. I needed to understand the science of that shit. What differentiated one muthafucka from another? What was the difference in the quality of their beats? Was their production considered rough or smooth? What type of voice sounded best on hardcore tracks? Whose voice was the most unique? Whose style was the most memorable? Sometimes when I got really high, I would listen to Tupac and I could feel the hairs on my arms rising. Tupac's fiery message was all passion and pride. Tupac's mom was a Black Panther and the rage and militancy that flowed through his veins inspired me.

I started studying in 1991 and have never stopped. It was as if I was in school and hip-hop was my major. I listened to all of the joints from the MCs that were at the top of their games. I was studying Dr. Dre, who was killing it with his funky head-bobbing joint, "Nuthin' But a G Thang" that featured another new nigga, Snoop Dogg. Dre's album was called *The Chronic* and the album just had a picture of Dre and a weed plant. Dre's style was a nice even flow and Snoop was the perfect partner because his flow was like molasses, slow and melodic. The track by Dr. Dre was strictly for head bobbing.

The West Coast MCs had a different flow from the East Coast. The West Coast was laid-back with their shit. It wasn't always about hustling. It was more about enjoying life in the hood. You could hear the sunshine in their tracks, which were funky and danceable. *The Chronic* was the muthafucking shit and when Snoop got on the track, people didn't know what to do. It was so different and so new. A year later when Snoop came out with his own shit, it was unforgettable. Hip-hop's bar had been raised.

Nas, Biggie Smalls, and Jay-Z from the East Coast were also showing me the power of the greats. I wanted to join them someday.

These artists were releasing the gold standard of albums which defined an era. Every time there was a new release, muthafuckas were on the edge of their seats. We never knew what to expect. Who would have the most ill sound, the most violent video, the most clever idea? We were celebrating the creative energy of the music.

IN SEPTEMBER 1996, it was all over the news. Tupac was dead. It had been a year since Brittney was born and things were moving along with my music. When I heard about his death on the news, I thought that it was some kind of a joke.

I remember the first time I met Tupac. It was at Queens' Day, which is a festival where they also have concerts. It's held in Flushing Meadows-Corona Park, where they have the 1964 World's Fair Unisphere. Tupac was performing and he was with some of my homies from around the way—Stretch, Madge and Nichols. Stretch and Madge were part of a group called Live Squad. I would always hear stories about all of them hanging with Pac on Hollis Avenue, but I had not gotten the chance to meet him. That day, it would all change. I saw Pac walking toward the stage. My friend Nichols was headed in the same direction and he introduced us. I shook his hand. I was happy to be in his presence and to meet him. Never could I have imagined that day, that one day, I would be mentioned in the same breath as Pac, even compared with him.

The next time I got a chance to see him was one night in The Tunnel, a legendary nightclub in Manhattan. He was there with Big. This was before all of the East Coast/West Coast beef. Tupac and Big were at the bar, and Pac had a line of women just wanting to touch him, be in his presence, or whatever. I remember thinking, *I want that. I want to be large like that.*

The death of Tupac shook us all to the bone. We had just lost Easy-E from NWA in March 1995 and death seemed to be creeping up on us as young Black men in the hood. Like I was telling Aisha, muthafuckas were getting killed every day around the block. Now, even famous young Black men like Easy-E. *But not Tupac.* He had sold 75 million albums worldwide. He was considered one of the bestselling artists in the world. He wrote songs that were reflecting the consciousness of Black people. Tupac was a chameleon. He knew how to adapt to his surroundings. He was hard and soft at the same time. His impact was powerful in the hood.

LOOKING BACK AT MY VERSE, I realized that Tupac was a fallen angel like I mentioned in my rhyme. He was a proud Black man and his passion for Black people, which I felt in his music, made me think long and hard about the neighborhood and the condition of our people.

Everyone was rhyming about the hood, but Tupac's shit made me think about it a little harder and a little deeper. Just seeing his face flash all over the TV screen with only twenty-five years between his birth date and his death date made me shiver. On a random day in September, the news of Tupac's death could have been the news of any one of ours: mine, Rich's or O's. It could have even been Gotti's. The hairs on my arms were standing again. I closed the notebook and went out on the fire escape to chill.

Neither Irv, Black nor O expressed anything to each other about Tupac's death except *"Damn."* We smoked a little extra weed and poured the ceremonial Hennessy out onto the concrete, into the cracks filled with emptied crack vials. Tupac was another reminder that in this so-called thug life no one was safe. Not even if you wanted to do the right thing, even if you were talented or famous. Fame couldn't hide from death. Not even if you just had a baby. . . .

AS I WALKED DOWN the street headed for the studio, I looked at how grayness shrouded everything around us, even though the sun was trying to shine. I stumbled over the concrete, which was only full of lost dreams. I looked around at the other people on the street. Some bruthas were smoking, some drunk, some hustling and some were ghosts because the drugs had won. All of them were scheming about how to get the next dollar or the next hit.

I thought about the fact that it wasn't so long ago that Black men were considered only three quarters of a man. Maybe, the problem is that we're all looking for the other quarter of ourselves. I heard Tupac's "So Many Tears" blasting out of a car stopped at a traffic light. The slow syrupy beat and low bass shook the car slightly.

Hip-hop was lifting the veil off of our pain. Hip-hop was our slave narrative. That's part of why the music is so powerful and has longevity. Not just the conscious songs, but the music as a whole. It is reflective of our reality, which is not all the same.

AS THE TRAIN NOISILY RAMBLED into the city I could hear my crew in my head. I could hear them chanting my new shit in unison with no music behind them. I wanted the sound to be stark and raw. I pulled out my tattered notebook and scribbled:

> *Yeah, been a slave too long*
> *All my murderers*
> *Let's march my niggas*
> *Lord can we get a break?*
> *Lord can we get a break?*
> *We ain't really happy here*
> *We ain't really happy here*
> *Take a look into our eyes*
> *Take a look into our eyes*
>
> *And see pain without fear*
> *And see pain without fear*

I knew Irv would love it, even though it wasn't even a rhyme, really. It's just something I wanted the world to hear. Ever since I saw *Glory* with Denzel Washington and Morgan Freeman, this shit had been ringing in my ears. In the movie, they were singing a battle hymn. Hip-hop needed its own, that's what gave me the idea.

Irv was standing outside. I told him of my idea of the battle hymn and he was with it. Irv trusted my instincts and I trusted his.

"It's dope. Let's make it the intro for the whole album. Niggas will go crazy! No one has done no shit like that!"

"Word," I said. *My* music was starting to happen.

SADLY, WE'RE TOO eager to throw ourselves out there, because we Black men don't see ourselves as living a long time. There is so much violence in our lives—whether we are watching it on television, witnessing a man beating on a woman in our own home, our homies getting shot—we get numb to it. In the hood, thirty-eight and thirty-nine are considered old. Most men don't make it to that age. Death is expected because of our experiences of young people dying around us. In the hood we say, "It get hot, somebody get shot." Our living conditions, past and present, from slavery to segregation, from the civil rights era to today's kids believing that racism doesn't exist (but can't identify where their sadness and lack of self-belief come from), make a lot of us believe that life isn't worth living. We need to start to respect and cherish ourselves and what we have to offer. This will allow us to learn to live, and expect to live long lives, and plan to live. Other races plan for tomorrow. They got 401(k)s and we're still trying to figure why we need that. We don't want to die and imagine someone else spending the money we saved. It's important to live long and live strong. And, it is a blessing to be able to leave something for the next generation.

*

July 22, 2011

I've reached the last spot on my Jail Tour. LOL. Midstate Correctional Facility, the best spot of them all. This is truly not jail, it's a camp. My first day was a feel-out process, like everywhere else kinda just getting use to my new surroundings. The inmates seem pretty cool. Most of them came up and introduced themselves like it was the first day of school or some shit. I was only back at Oneida for 2 days after coming back from court and the dreaded Green Monster. Speaking of court, I finally had my day and I can gratefully say I am happy wit the verdict. It felt like days sitting in the back in the holding cell waiting to come out, like a lion trapped in his cage when he should be out in the wild roaming free. That's just how I felt, like an animal, as they brought me out in my yellow Fed jumpsuit, chained up hands and feet. I could barely walk. As I enter, doing the old jailhouse shuffle, I look out into the courtroom full of reporters and news people. I spot Ish. Her face was all puffy eyes, red and swollen. I could tell she's been crying. I look to her side and see my Mom with the same face. I felt like a piece of shit. I look further down and see Tina, BJ and Gutta. BJ and Gutta was smiling and that made me feel a lil better. Men have a funny way of communicating even though this was no smiling or laughing matter. I knew what the smiles meant—hold your head, my man, this too shall pass. But the moment couldn't be more real. Those tears in Ish and my Moms eyes were because they knew what I knew, that I could get 36 more months ran consecutive. The moment of truth was upon us all. As the proceedings started, everything went silent for me for a moment. All I could hear was my own thoughts. I was thinking about how I'm letting everyone down, my family, my friends, my fans. Then I heard the words that melted my cold heart, "daughter's graduation." My body became unnumb and finally a tear rolled down my left cheek. I thought for sure there was no way I was gonna get out in time now, to see my daughter graduate. The hurt turned into anger and more tears started to flow. I look at the judge. She looks unmoved by Stacy's testimony. I had to do something. The only thing I can do is speak before the court. I wipe the tears and prepared what I wanted to say in my head. Then I spoke, still a little choked up, I said my peace. The judge looked at me intently, as I spoke from the heart. She felt my pain and sentenced me 28 months to run concurrent wit my current conviction. THAT WAS LOVE. I'll be home in time to see Britt graduate, THANK GOD.

*

EIGHT

---

160 Varick

IRV, O AND I HAD SAT IN THE LOBBY OF DEF JAM FOR FORTY-five minutes, not saying a word. "How can he have us waiting all this time? To hell with this guy. I'm not waiting any longer," Gotti finally burst, as he stood up to leave. "If he doesn't think that we're important enough to meet, I'm out!"

Desperate to calm him down, I said, "The man wants to meet us. That's why we're here. He may have gotten delayed with some other business, but he *invited* us. I'm sure that—"

Just as I was buying more time, his assistant, Kat, suddenly appeared in the lobby to get us. She was an older white lady who was really sweet.

"Lyor wants to see you now. Sorry for the wait," she said as she led us down a long hallway to Lyor Cohen's office, which sat at the end of the hall with an enormous picture window with a breathtaking view of Manhattan from the twentieth floor.

I could see workers on both sides of us as we made our way down the hallway to the corner office. Assistants on the left in gray steel cubicles and executives in their glass offices on the right. Both sides were blasting their favorite joints. The energy was raw and real. You could hear the thick beats of the Def Jam roster thumping out of every office: Method Man, Redman, EPMD.

I was a kid in a candy store. I wanted to touch, feel, smell and hear everything that was swirling around me. The stench of weed seeped out of everyone's gear, 'fros, and 'locs. The Def Jam office was filled with the sleek shine of stainless steel and the ruggedness of exposed brick walls. In every corner of the office, young Black men were holding up walls, some sitting, some standing, all listening to Def Jam's newest joints.

"Please! That shit's wack, that's why Def Jam didn't sign him!" one guy would say.

"This style is crazy, yo!" someone else called out.

All around the floor you could hear the opinions and love for hip-hop. They were arguing and defending their favorite MCs or trashing the beats that didn't hold up. Some bounced shamelessly to the sounds that wouldn't let them sit still.

Only a place like Def Jam could sell *millions* of records. Def Jam wasn't just making hip-hop, they were re-creating culture. The souls of Black people were in the room. Everyone's head was bobbing as they worked, getting knee-deep in hip-hop. This was the first time I'd ever felt the power of youth in my heart. This was the only place where young Black men could just be who they were and still be treated with respect.

The rip of cardboard boxes being opened sliced the air. Boxes of new product, promotional T-shirts and posters came in a steady stream throughout the day. The assistants were stripping down so that they could put on the newest shirts, fresh from the boxes. The interns mounted posters of their favorite artists while the boxes with the vinyl were being sorted to be shipped to the best club DJs around the country. There was even a pile labeled "International."

I was surprised to see Bimy from back in the day opening up boxes. He was A&Ring at Def Jam. I hadn't seen him in a while. Everyone was trying to be down with hip-hop in any way they could. Bimy hustled mainly, but liked hanging around the business in case an opportunity popped up. Bimy couldn't rap at all but he wanted to be down with the industry, nonetheless. Bimy saw me and greeted me with a "What up." The look on his face showed that he was impressed to see me there, walking towards Lyor's office.

You could see each worker mouthing the words to their favorite joints as the joints spilled out of the speakers. The walls, already covered with posters, were redressed in order to make room for the newest posters, without taking anyone down. Every image was bigger than life, just like the music. *This is what I'm talking about* . . . Def Jam was where I belonged.

On the real, it was my dream in living color. I had never been inside of Def Jam, but I knew this is how it would be. Hip-hop was electrifying everything it touched. My rhymes were no longer something that I wanted to keep to myself or keep in the studio or even share with my homies on the block.

Hip-hop was all about fearlessness, attitude and Black rage that the world hadn't even seen yet. Hip-hop was revolution. Hip-hop was daring the world to be down with *us*, despite how the industry tried to censor us. Everyone knew what was up. *Finally*, something was about young Black men and what *we* saw, what *we* thought and most importantly how we *felt*.

RUSSELL SIMMONS AND LYOR COHEN were industry legends. Lyor was a tall, gangly Jewish kid who emigrated from Israel to America and Russell was a middle-class Black kid from Queens who loved music. Lyor's piercing blue eyes, loud voice and bumpy Israeli accent startled most people at first, but he knew his shit. Even though Cohen was white, he was just like the Haitian and the Jamaican immigrants that flooded America, looking for all that America had to offer. He was an outsider just like everyone else, but found his home in the beats like we all did. Although Lyor had studied global marketing and finance, he was smart but also determined to move Black culture into the mainstream. Russell's laid-back persona, million-dollar smile and his unique talent of bridging the gap between cultures made him an icon. Hip-hop was considered on the fringes because of the street element. Russell brought it mainstream and made it highly commercial. Russell seemed meek with his whispery tone, yet he was a powerhouse, not to be fucked with.

It was the genius of Russell and Lyor combined that made it possible to pair rappers up with mainstream brands like Adidas and Coke and make it edgy but still cool. That shit was unbelievable to me, that America was ready to let young Black people sell them shit.

Lyor Cohen knew exactly what he wanted. It never mattered what anyone else wanted—and that's how he ran his business. His loud, incomprehensible rants, throwing papers in the faces of his staff and pounding his fists on desks made him infamous. "It's not good enough!" "Do it again!" "You spent how much?" Thrown and broken phones became his trademark. When he would slam down a phone or throw it across a room, he would always end his calls with, "And, fuck you!" Every MC wanted to be down with Def Jam, no matter what they heard. The roster was filling up fast. The only true competition in hip-hop for me existed inside these walls.

Hip-hop was the new legal drug. As if it were the new sheriff in town, everyone treated it with respect and placed the type of value on it that America hadn't seen since the beginning of Motown. Hip-hop was threatening life as we knew it. The raw pain of urban America was no longer a secret, the music was real time. What we were rapping about was actually happening in the streets and *the truth hurts.* The millions of records that Def Jam was selling every week had the other labels scratching their heads.

White people were becoming terrified because their children were showing the ultimate sign of rebellion, by listening to hip-hop and *wanting* to be like niggas. Rappers were irreverent and suddenly seductive. Young white boys wanted to be us and little white girls wanted to *fuck* us. At that time, everyone was fiending for a piece of hip-hop. Every music executive desperately needed to get in some way or other. Lyor Cohen had people to see and deals to make.

It was 1996 and I was nineteen years old. I was confident that after this meeting, Lyor would have the power to end the TVT nightmare. He was known for being a cutthroat mutha-fucka. And if it all went right, I would be the next MC walk-ing these halls with a poster of myself behind everyone's desk. When we finally reached Lyor's office, he offered us some water but we declined because we were eager to get right into it. Lyor sat back in his chocolate brown leather chair, looked at us squarely and said, "I only want the little guy."

No one knew what to say. He was clear, but what he was saying, none of us was trying to hear. For seconds, which felt like minutes, the sound of the beats from the hall had ceased. There was only the loud buzz of Lyor's cell phone, which was on vibrate. He didn't answer it. I was "the little guy," and what Lyor was saying was that O was out of the picture. Lyor saw a future for me at Def Jam. *Only me.* What would I say to O when we walked out of there? The dream was on, but it was starting on a fucking awkward note.

Gotti took the meeting from there. Gotti was already standing up, leaning in, over Lyor's desk. Gotti was speaking fast about his new shit.

"Lyor, if you give me a chance I won't disappoint you. I have the hot shit. Ja Rule is only the beginning. I know a hit when I hear it." I watched as Gotti sealed the deal, pointing his fingers and flailing his arms. Lyor slid his hand across the smooth leather desk, silent but giddy with anticipation of the millions he was about to make.

As a new artists and repertoire (A&R) guy for Def Jam, Irv would be able to bring all of his artists to Def Jam.

After Gotti said his piece, Lyor said, "You have until the end of the day to make a decision on what I've offered. The little guy and you, Irv. Come back before six with your answer. I'll have the papers ready for you to sign." Lyor spoke as though O wasn't even there. It was the first sign to me that Lyor was cold-blooded. O was crushed, but he did what men do, he said nothing. When we got out on the street, the three of us walked in silence. I thought about how I would feel if it happened to me—if they selected O and didn't want me. But, really, it had nothing to do with either of us, or so I told myself. I was just what Def Jam was looking for at the time. A different day could have been O's day.

"Yo. That's all right. Rule, I give you my blessing. You go 'hed and do that shit and you and I will get back to it another time," O said.

WE TOOK THE DEAL but Steve Gottlieb and Lyor Cohen had reached an impasse. Irv got a full-time job with benefits at the best hip-hop label in the world and I still couldn't get out of my deal with TVT. Steve would not let me go, and Lyor still wanted me but he didn't have time to wait for me. Lyor needed a big act to take the ride on the platinum path that he would lay out. Time never waits when you got paper to make. Steve Gottlieb was blocking my shit. All I could do was sit and wait for my own five-year sentence to end, just like Black's. When anyone signs a group deal, it forever solidifies that relationship. This means that if something happens to one person in the group, it impacts everyone in the group. I learned that it is important to make sure that my individual creative rights are protected.

WHILE I WAS IN A HOLDING PATTERN, waiting for Steve Gottlieb to realize that Cash Money Click was no longer, Lyor had no choice but to sign DMX. DMX's first album sold five million records and 250,000 copies in the first week. "Ruff Ryder's Anthem," which was a collaboration with X's crew, was also a hit, selling another five million copies. DMX's people were The Lox, Drag-On, and another female MC, Eve. Gotti could do no wrong.

I first met X in Mulford Gardens. It was a crazy project to live in. I couldn't believe people actually lived like that. The windows were all broken out. It was crazy. X was rhyming. He had recently gotten beat up, so his jaw was wired shut. While he was rapping, the wires were popping out everywhere. We were all spitting. Me, Lox and X. Afterward, when I was done rhyming, X said, "Little nigga, get busy." It is important to know that X don't usually give it up to no one. He's a tough give. At the time, though, the compliment didn't mean much to me because X wasn't famous yet. He was popular on the streets. X was a mixed-tape legend in Yonkers. When X first got signed to Def Jam, folks were joking, "Who is going to buy his album—dogs!" Whenever he went to the offices at the label, he would bring his two dogs inside. He was a loose cannon, but he came out and smashed it.

DMX was a good dude, and a good friend, but the drugs changed him. He was doing all kinds of shit, like missing shows, video shoots and interviews.

I remember one time I got locked up because of X. We were recording at Quad. We came back from the store. A guy downstairs was selling watches.

"What you doing with my brother's watch? That's my brother's watch right there," X said.

Next thing I knew, X knocked the guy out and robbed the guy for the watches. He was famous. Why was he robbing people? While we were trying to get upstairs, back into the studio, the watch guy was downstairs calling the police. The receptionist warned us that the police were on their way up just in case we had weed or something. X hid behind the reel to reel. I was like, I gotta get the fuck out of here. I b-line for the stairs because I thought the police would be coming up in the elevator. As I made my move, I saw that they were coming up the stairs and were on the elevator. The police had the watch guy with them. As they run into me, they ask the watch guy who robbed him.

"Is this one of the guys that robed you?" the police asked, as they ran into me.

"Yes, him, right there."

The police had their man. They were going to look no further. X hid and I went to central booking. When I called Irv, at Def Jam, they came and got me from the precinct.

That's just one of me and X's escapades. Another time we were out in Miami. My music was out, so we were both big. We were down there for a music conference. X wanted to go and get some weed. The man drives like a maniac. He believes he has to beat everybody on the road. There are millions of cars on the road, and he thinks he has to beat every one of them. It's like he's in a race. The police pull us over.

"This ain't really my car. It's Keizer's car," X says.

"All that sound good, but ya'll ain't going nowhere in this car. It is not registered to you."

"That's cool. Whatever," X said, as he got out of the car. "Don't worry Rule, I got this."

Standing on the side of the highway, X proceeds to stick out his thumb. Immediately, a girl stops. She is so excited that she takes us to her mother's house to brag. Her mama wanted to cook us food.

Gotti had a vision for me, X and Jay-Z to be a supergroup. I went on the road with X. Next, Def Jam sent me to France with Redman, Method Man and Onyx. We were freestyling on the radio and no one spoke English. Those French guys who were at the station were freestyling right along with us. They were dope. We didn't understand what we were saying but their flow was right on point. That experience showed me that we were making art. We could feel it. And they felt us, too.

THE OTHER NEW KID, Shawn Carter from Brooklyn, who called himself Jay-Z, wore a New York Yankees baseball cap on his head. He wore a crisp white T-shirt and a leather jacket and Tims. Plain as he was, he just looked successful. It was hard to explain. His confidence was unforgettable. Damon Dash and Biggs were his partners at the start-up label, Roc-A-Fella Records. Jay-Z was a flashy guy with big ideas and a bigger ego.

Jay-Z thought that the only way to get things done was with dough. He had already had success with his first indie release, *Reasonable Doubt.* Jay-Z was curious about how to get his record played at radio stations across the country. Gotti told him that the best radio guy in the business was Kevin Liles and suggested that he go see him.

"What the fuck is this? Is it Christmas?" Liles asked him.

Jay-Z had admired Def Jam's radio domination. He wanted that for his own label. He thought the loot was going to get him what he wanted. They all laughed. "It doesn't work like that, man," Liles told him and then he explained how shit did work.

I had written a song for my solo album called "Can I Get A . . ." Jay-Z liked that shit and asked if he could have it. I thought that would be okay as long as he let me be on the track and in the video. In exchange, Jay-Z agreed to do a record on my album, "Kill 'Em All." "Can I Get A . . ." turned out to be a big hit partly because it went on the *Rush Hour* soundtrack.

IRV WAS PRIMING ME for my own album to drop the following year by having me work with Jay-Z and DMX. It was a win-win. For me, it was my coming-out party, and for Jay-Z, it was a big radio smash.

With the guest appearance on "Can I Get A . . ." I was able to start doing appearances with Jay-Z. The first time we performed that song, it was at the Tunnel. Everything was coming full circle. Not too long ago, I had been at the Tunnel watching Big and Pac. Now, here I was about to perform a record with Jay-Z. I had no idea Jay-Z would do that record that night. He was doing "22 Two's" and then he went to "Can I Get A . . ." He waves at me to come up on the stage. There were so many people between me and the stage. I wasn't sure if I could get to it. Next thing I know, my friend BJ picked me up, and the crowd passed me to the stage like a blunt. When I got on stage, the spotlight I was longing for was finally mine.

The local clubs loved that shit, having two of their own MCs that had a record coming out to perform live.

The club was crowded and the fans gave us mad love. The first time I did a show with Jay-Z was like a blur. Aisha was extremely excited for me. I remember her faith in me clearly. I smoked an extra blunt, drank and got nice. My dream was about to come true. Even though I was on someone else's stage, it felt like my own.

The video shoot for "Can I Get A . . ." was cool. It was in another club in Manhattan and it was packed with everyone dressed up like it was a party even though it was ten in the morning. The video was a collage of images of Jay-Z and Amil and some fly-ass dancers intercut with scenes from *Rush Hour* with Chris Tucker and Jackie Chan. I was sprinkled throughout the video and did a verse. Everything was going great with the video, except I didn't have my own identity. I was seen as "the guy with J."

"I see you back there doing pushups in the back. What are you like under there?" the director Brett Ratner asked, referring to my six pack.

"I'm all right."

"Why don't you do a take with no shirt?"

At first I was hesitant, I thought I looked great in my new flashy clothes. But the problem was they didn't give me no presence.

When the video aired, everybody wanted to know who was the rapper at the end of the video. Me. In essence, taking off my shirt was the best thing I could have ever done. That was the night I became Ja Rule, not the guy on J's record. It gave me an identity. After that I don't think I ever put on a shirt again.

The film was directed by Brett Ratner, who was a young Jewish kid who had been doing hip-hop videos until he got his big break directing movies like *Money Talks* with Chris Tucker and then *Rush Hour*. He was another young guy doing his thing, which made me all the more impatient. It was difficult watching other talented people get theirs. I was happy to see them make moves because it meant I was in the right place, associating with the right people. It was challenging being patient.

Luckily, the *Rush Hour* soundtrack was a hit and I was slowly becoming somebody. It was so close I could taste it.

I WAS LATER OFFERED A ROLE in a movie, *Turn It Up,* with Pras from the Fugees. Doing the movie meant a good little paycheck. It was about the drug game and the music game. It wasn't a stretch because I had lived the shady shit that goes down with the music industry and the streets and understood how the two are always connected.

Right before my album dropped in 1999, we were about to go out on the Hard Knock Life Tour. We all felt good about the album, except I didn't have a single that could be played on the radio. A hot single playing on the radio helps to draw attention to albums. One of the producers came to me with a slamming beat. I listened to it for a bit then came up "Holla Holla." This is where my double flow comes from. It was Jimmy Two Times from *A Bronx Tale* that planted the concept in me. Yeah, yeah . . . I couldn't believe it but I was actually going on tour with the MCs that I'd been admiring for years. The legendary Hard Knock Life Tour in 1999 included DMX, Jay-Z, Redman, Method Man, Beanie Sigel, DJ Clue?, Memphis Bleek and Amil. They even made a documentary about that shit called *Backstage*. This was the first hip-hop tour since Fresh Fest in 1984. It was fifteen years between the two tours. Until Hard Knock, arenas were not willing to pay the high price of insurance to secure hip-hop acts and audience. That's why it was a big deal. We preached to our crowds to keep it clean.

THE TOUR WAS UNBELIEVABLE. I can't even express what it's like to have twenty thousand muthafuckas a night, in fifty cities across the country, come to check us out. I'll always remember the powerful impact it had on me to be standing on a stage looking down at kids of all colors who knew every lyric we spit. It was life-changing for all of us because we were getting the mad *love* we had missed in our hard-knock-life realities. Almost everywhere you look, and everything you read, tells you that Black men ain't nothing. But, when we're on that stage it's not true. When we're on that stage, everybody wants to be us and be with us.

As time went on and I was on stage more and more, the feeling became more and more powerful. It gave me an incredible charge. I felt invincible, loved. I was Superman. I was on top of the world. When I had all of these people I didn't know screaming my name, or whatever I told them to holler, it played with my mind. "Throw your hands up! Say, 'Yeah, yeah!'" This is how the industry creates its egomaniacs. It's how Kanye West can say that he's God. I get it. I understand the feeling. But people are not comfortable with a Black man calling himself God. But, we're taught in the Bible that we're made in His image. And how we should live our lives in accordance with God's words. So, what's wrong with Kanye saying that. Aren't we all God's children. Our gifts are a blessing, but it's up to us to use them productively, and not take them for granted or even abuse them.

Being onstage made me want to live, too. Most Black men think that we're going to die young, because that's what we see around us—a lot of unnecessary killing. Performing affirmed my life. It gave me more of a reason to want to live.

After coming off the Hard Knock Life Tour, it was time to shoot my second single, "Murda 4 Life." We shot it on Jamaica Avenue. The whole hood came out to support. The video was originally suppose to feature Memphis Bleek, but for some reason he wasn't cleared to do the video. Which never made sense to me considering we were all under the same umbrella. He was on Roc-A-Fella and I was on Murder Inc. Both were subsidiaries of Def Jam. We ended up putting Black Child and

Cadillac Tah on the record. During the shooting of the video, 50 showed up. According to him, he came to say "What's up?" to me, and I didn't show him enough love. I gave him a "what up" and kept it moving. I think he was jealous because Black Child was on the record and not him. The hood was showing me love and not him. Shortly after, he recorded a diss record about me, "Murder, I Don't Believe You." This is how it all started.

"Your man got a song about me. What's up with your man?" I asked Black Child.

"Yeah, I heard about it. I don't fuck with that nigga," said Black Child. "But, when I see him, I'm going to holla at him."

The next time Black saw 50 he asked him what's up with the record. 50 said, "Ain't no hard feelings. It's just a record. I'm trying to get me out there." He was basically copping pleas. I didn't think nothing else about it.

August 30, 2011

I've been down now going on 4 months, another 16 to go. I'm not gonna lie I hate this shit. I hate being told what to do, when to go to bed, when I can go outside. I feel like I'm 10 years old again, LOL. But I'm in a good headspace, been studying to take my GED. I haven't been to school in like 15 years. You'd be amazed at all the shit you forget in that time, especially math. But I'm getting it done. I'm mad and sad I'm not home wit the family these past few weeks wit all that's been going on, the earthquake, Hurricane Irene. This shit doesn't happen normally on the East Coast. I was worried about Ish and the kids. Thank God we didn't get hit that hard in my area and everyone is safe. The week before my grandmother, Bruce and Dawn came to see me wit Ish and my Mom. I was glad they came. I had a good time talking about old times and the family. I learned a lot about my family and I'm not the first to be in prison, but hopefully I will be the last. My Moms hip was looking real bad on the visit. The doctor said she's gonna need a hip replacement. She's a lil scared. I spoke to her a few days ago and she started crying. I love my Mom and we're really close. She's very sensitive. I told her there's nothing to be scared of and not to worry, she'll be running in no time. LOL. It made her feel better. she said she was also sad that she wouldn't be able to see me for a while. But for me her health is all that matters.

I watched MTV Awards Sunday. It was cool. I think LaLa had the best performance. Music is just not the same without me. LOL. Can't wait to get out and record. Fuck Fame, my last album. I'm gonna make it a double, then I think I should retire. After seeing how everyone was dressed at the awards, I think I'm getting too old for this shit. LOL. HOLLYWOOD HERE I COME! And I'm bringing Britt wit me.

*

NINE

What's Beef?

IT WAS 1999, I WAS TWENTY-THREE YEARS OLD AND MY FIRST joint, *Venni Vetti Vecci,* was out. We were number two on the charts, and I had a huge radio hit, "Holla Holla," which was blasting out of every car on the streets and keeping the CD on the list. I had just released my second single, "Murda 4 Life." (*Venni Vetti Vecci* went on to sell 2 million copies total, but the interesting thing is that the first week it came out, it sold 187,000 copies, and 187 is the LA police code for murder. Me and Irv Gotti thought it was a sign from God that our time had come. It's murder had finally become a reality.)

Hell yeah, *I came, I saw and I conquered.*

Gotti's strategy had always been to share a little of each of his hot rappers on everybody's joints so we would all benefit from the repeat name recognition. At that time, all of Irv's artists had nothing but love and respect for each other. We all came up together. We were all selling albums, doing shows and we were all getting paid. But that didn't seem to be enough.

It only took a year for my man DMX to accuse me of sounding like him. In 2000, he wrote a diss joint called "Do You," which insinuated that I was copying his style. Truth is, the only similarity between us is that we both had gruff voices—but that was the only similarity. I'm *nothing* like him.

Word of the beef between us spread quickly throughout the hip-hop community, but to be honest, I was too busy working on my second album to care. Making music was my dream and I was in it to win it.

During this period I went through a transformation. People were saying that I acted like Pac and sounded like X. Here is when I realized that I'm me. I'm an artist and had to express myself as an artist, and do me. My whole sound was kind of different. My first album was street because that's all I knew up to that point. But after the first album, I was living success.

When I presented my second album, *Rule 3:36,* to Def Jam, they learned the hard way that I was going to push the envelope.

When I refused to do my second album over, Def Jam pushed back and I pushed even harder. At first they were only going to release the single "Between Me and You" with no video or anything and see how it would move. Me and Gotti wasn't having none of that. We had just sold a gang of records; how could they not give me a proper release? Eventually they caved and gave me the kind of rollout I had earned—video budget, radio spend, street team. It proved my instincts had been right. *Rule 3:36* came out and went triple platinum, 3 million records, sold nearly 300,000 the first week. *You couldn't tell me nothing.*

Ja Rule and Murder Inc. were slaying the radio. Our joints added the instrumentation of R&B and the sensuality of female vocals and put them over dope rap tracks. The combination made every hot joint even hotter.

As Murder Inc. continued to grow, we came to realize that we had crossed an invisible line. By switching up the same ol' formula for hip-hop and adding these other elements, we'd gone outside of the boundary lines. The underground fans didn't like it. The critics criticized. The bloggers blogged. The fighters fought. And rappers wrote diss records about us. They were all trying to hit us where it hurt most—our commitment to the authenticity of the music and our manhood. While that was happening, the larger population was eating us up. Inside the business there was lots of scrutiny, outside, lots of love.

The beef inside the hip-hop community was everywhere. The barbs flew across the radio airwaves while the Internet broke the dam of public opinion. Every day there were hundreds of never-ending anonymous comments that fueled the fires.

LIKE I SAID, me and DMX came up together. When my music started to blow up as large as his, I believe that's the moment that people started getting in X's ear. They were provoking him by saying shit like, "That little homie is trying to steal your shit" or "He's trying to be like you." Those comments triggered him. Actually, I think it was really Lyor who was provoking us to compete against each other, he'd say to me, "J's in the studio working." He'd say to X, Ya know Ja's album just went number one." I don't think he meant any malice; he just wanted us to create new music and bring in more money.

When I look back on it, I realize that I had become a red flag not just for X, but for several others. It's like hustling on a block and here comes a new guy who is coming up after you. He *may* be the guy to kill you or your business.

All of this stuff, the tension between artists, is very personal. We're mostly from the same area. We have similar dreams and similar skill sets. We're competing against each other, while also using the other for inspiration. When it looks like someone may overshadow us, our ego gets in the way and the disrespect begins. We are fighters and survivors. We can't take disrespect. We have zero tolerance.

The next time I see 50 is in Atlanta.

In 2000, I got a call to do a show. The opening act was to be 50 Cent. The promoter who booked us didn't know that 50 had some issues with me. When I pulled up to the hotel, I was surprised to see my man Uncle Chaz. He had started managing 50 Cent. Chaz asked if I'd talk to 50 to squash any beef that was brewing. I agreed to it. A few minutes later 50 pulls up. We get to talking. He's copping more pleas: "It's nothing personal. It's just me trying to get out there. The record's already out there, it's not going anywhere. Nothing we can do about it." I don't know why, but that set me off. I started screaming on him. Calling him a bitch ass nigga. With every album he tries to beef with someone to get people to start talking about him and to create a buzz for his album. I wish he would stop trying to use gimmicks and concentrate on the music.

Rage started to bubble up in my stomach. Although my intentions were to talk, I couldn't help myself, I just started screaming on him.

50 tried to swing on me, but I dipped, then I hit him with the baby Louisville Slugger. Bam! I dropped the bat. I pulled the shirt over his head. I started catching him, left, right, uppercut. Then O comes and picks up the bat and starts cracking him over the head. Black Child joins in and hits him, too. We were fucking him up and none of his people did anything. The OGs, BJ and Uncle Chaz broke it up.

The funny thing about that Atlanta shit is that when my crew started smashing him, 50's crew ran inside the hotel and got on the elevator. I was still heated. I took the ashtray stand from outside and brought it into the hotel lobby, hoping to crack it over anybody's head that was in my way. As the elevator door closed, I threw the ashtray stand. The staff called the police. My last words to him were, "Nigga you better not show up tonight. Or you will die."

We had done enough that day. The crew and I bounced and did our show, without an opening act. No one knew who the fuck 50 was at that time, so no one missed him.

By the time I got back to New York, I heard that 50 had woven a ridiculous fictional tale about the Atlanta incident. He deserved another ass whooping just for that.

On March 20, I got a call from a friend who happened to be hanging out at the Hit Factory studio in New York City. "Guess who's in the studio tonight?" she asked. I thanked her for the tip. I knew what I had to do. My man Merc, he had broken his foot. I took his crutch to use as a weapon. I was headed upstairs, because I happened to be at the Hit Factory that night, too. My crew followed me. We paid 50 Cent a visit. He was still talking, rhyming and talking too much shit with his silly mouth. That incident in Atlanta showed me that the beef had just begun. I was getting mad.

Not knowing which studio suite 50 was in, we went from door to door until we found him. I opened the door and 50 was in a small recording studio. He was inches from me. He looked at me like he had seen a ghost.

He said, "Yo, let's talk."

"You been talking enough." BAM! I pushed my way into the studio. I hit him with the crutch. We proceeded to whip his ass. I was putting in my work. 50 was crunched in the corner. I slammed the big Tannoy speaker down on him.

While he's getting his ass beat, I heard him say, "Get the gun."

"Get your gun, nigga," I replied.

At that moment, Black started poking niggas with a knife, and 50 got stabbed. After blood was shed, we got out of there.

I had had it with 50 Cent. I wanted to hurt his ass. He needed to be silenced. I needed to show him who he was playing with. I felt that I had to defend what I'd worked so hard for, for all those years. I was defending my reputation and my art. I wasn't going to let someone come in and desecrate my music with those ridiculous diss records and stories. I was wearing my emotions on my sleeve. We all were. The rap shit was the first thing I had ever *owned*. It was something that I created and could claim as my own. It meant *everything* to me. I was young and reckless and didn't give a fuck. Every attack felt personal.

When I feel the tightening of my skin and the quickening pace of my heartbeat, it always leads to severe bodily harm for others. When provoked, there is no turning me off. That's what Moms used to say about my father.

In 2000, 50 Cent was still considered an underground artist with his leaked diss joints and unreleased Columbia Records album. He had a deal with Columbia Records but he was dropped before they could put the record out because of all the shit that he started.

In 50's mind the only way to get at me was to make records dissing me. I wasn't really worried about retaliating with diss records. I was making hits, so small-time disses that couldn't be played on the radio were not my concern. While he was dissing me, I was smashing the world with my success.

50 Cent's beef with me was no regular beef. It had been building for years. 50 was a crazed man on a mission to destroy me, specifically, as well as everything I had.

Preme and Chaz had seen enough. They were the OG's in the neighborhood. They called a meeting. Preme was to bring me to the meeting. Chaz was to get 50 there. We all agreed to the meeting, or so I thought. We met at Chaz's Blackhand studio. The three of us were alone, waiting on 50. Chaz was mad that 50 was late. He called 50 several times and 50 didn't pick up. Finally, he picks up.

Chaz says, "Where the fuck you at?" He was angry.

"I'm not coming. It's a setup. Ya'll is going to try and kill me," 50 said.

Chaz was offended. He let 50 know that if Chaz told him to come somewhere, he was safe. He wasn't going to let anything happen to him. No one was trying to kill him.

"I'm not coming. I don't trust ya'll. I don't feel safe," said 50.

Chaz hung up the phone.

I laughed, thinking 50's a real clown. "This is a waste of my time." I was out.

Shortly after that, 50 recorded the infamous record "Ghetto Qu'ran."

When I heard about "Ghetto Qu'ran," I couldn't believe the detail with which he snitched on Preme. Even I took that shit personally. The underground started to talk about 50 negatively. Muthafuckas realized that he should be avoided at all costs.

The word was out, 50 Cent is a snitch. "Ghetto Qu'ran" was to have serious repercussions. 50 Cent was in danger. When Preme heard about "Ghetto Qu'ran," the message was sent to every record producer and DJ throughout America not to play 50's shit and not to even fuck with him. The streets obeyed. At one point, 50 Cent couldn't even find a recording studio anywhere that would let him record in their facility.

During those early days 50 Cent was still trying to get on and having some trouble because of the ban. He was known as being combative and ruthless with nothing to lose. In many of his joints, the message was always the same, "fuck you" or "fuck it." That was all he ever had to say. He was all about disrespect. That's what I didn't like about him.

50 didn't get the warning. He came after *me* in joint after joint. I heard that he was constantly talking smack about us

and mentioning me in his songs every chance he got. 50 Cent really overdid it with the diss records.

Two months after the Hit Factory beatdown, 50 Cent went to visit his grandmother and was shot nine times outside of her house. 50 Cent filed a restraining order. He conveniently told the Feds that he feared for his life. While he was in the hospital, the police were working on him to give them information.

The Feds were back on the case, probing him about who he thought shot him. The Feds probably told him that he shouldn't go back on the streets without protection. When they asked him who he thought had shot him, it would make sense that 50 would have said, "Ja Rule, Irv Gotti and Murder Inc." I'm sure they told him, "We can help you get these guys."

50's in the hospital following my success. During this time, my album *Rule 3:36* is taking off. I'm touring the world. The sales reached 4 million, worldwide.

50 was healing for close to a year or more with all types of tubes and IVs pumping steroids into his body after taking all of those bullets. 50 Cent ended up being picked up by Eminem and his label, Shady Records, under Dr. Dre. This was significant because 50 Cent was from the East Coast and he was joining a West Coast crew. They made another diss record about me, but since The Inc. was under federal indictment, there was nothing that I could say. His debut album, which he must have been planning in his hospital bed, was called *Get Rich or Die Tryin'*, which is what he set out to do, at all costs.

From my perspective, the Feds worked their magic on 50 during this period. Although he says he "refused to cooperate with them," he secretly led them through his recordings for the answers they were looking for. It was already in the Feds' mind that Murder Inc. was behind all of this, and that McGriff had indeed funded Murder Inc. in exchange for making it seem that he had a legitimate career in music. I don't know where they would get that from. Preme's involvement in the Murder Inc. film *Crime Partners* was documented evidence that he was becoming legitimate. He had given two million dollars to fund the movie. That's what the money-laundering charges were based on. But Murder Inc. never gave Preme the money. At that point, the Feds believed they had a case that included drug money and an attempted murder, which could finally support a legitimate case with the district attorney.

50 Cent then hired a twenty-four-hour security brigade which included a core team of six men, several who had been former secret service. The price tag for that security was $50,000 a week.

THE BEEF WAS IMPACTING everything in hip-hop on the East Coast. Chris Lighty, RIP, had been Lyor Cohen's man for many years. Lighty was a former rapper turned executive who got in with Lyor and headed up Violator Records under Def Jam. He managed Busta Rhymes, Mobb Deep and Noreaga. During that period, Violator was so hot that no one could touch Chris Lighty. Lighty was also 50 Cent's manager. Chris Lighty had held the position with Lyor and with Def Jam that Irv Gotti was gaining on. In other words, Irv was quickly gaining stature.

Lyor and Lighty had a good relationship but it started to fall apart because Lyor's allegiances were shifting towards Gotti, which felt like a personal rejection to Chris. Gotti became Lyor's man, heralding in a new brigade of hip-hop artists that were maybe a little edgier than what had once been considered edgy. Gotti and Lyor were connected by their passion. They shared a vision of what could be if Gotti was put in the top position.

Russell Simmons even tried to call a meeting with Chris Lighty and Gotti to try to smooth over the beef, which was becoming a national scandal. Nothing happened, Gotti and Lighty just fought in front of Russell until he sent them both away.

On an even higher level, the music executive Doug Morris was running the whole thing from above. We were just puppets on his string. Morris was preparing to step down and eyes were on Jimmy Iovine or Lyor Cohen to take over Morris' multimillion-dollar position. Who was going to get the top spot? Jimmy Iovine represented Dr. Dre, Eminem and 50 Cent. Lyor Cohen represented Ja Rule and Murder Inc., DMX and Jay-Z. The rumor was that it was taken care of in the corporate way. Someone fanned the fire that created our downfall. They did it all with just a couple of phone calls. No fights, no bullets, no harsh words.

Someone made calls to MTV and BET and then calls were made to us. "We love you guys at Murder Inc. but this year Eminem will be performing at the MTV Awards. The artists don't feel safe with you in the building."

It was official. Murder Inc. had been banned from the spot-light.

This beef was far more colossal than the petty feuds that were reported in the news about Murder Inc. This was about warring factions. There were millions of dollars and endless possibilities for the future of hip-hop at stake.

"HOUSTON, WE HAVE A PROBLEM," is what Irv had said to me when we first heard the horns of "In da Club." The house that Irv and I had built was falling down. It was 2003. We both knew 50's shit was *hot*. People were talking about it everywhere. We both knew it was going to be a major problem for Murder Inc. For years we had been crushing everything in sight, it had been like a Ja Rule holiday. Maybe it was time for someone else to get a shot, but not *him,* not 50. The beef between 50 and me was all over the news. Murder Inc. had been shut down, the Feds had seized our shit and discredited our company and my reputation was all fucked-up.

What the fuck? It was all happening so fast that I couldn't even catch a brick as the walls of my life were coming down. I just had to brace myself. It was the cold, gritty water of hip-hop being thrown all over me. I was totally confused. 50 Cent was accusing me of something that he would eventually do on some of his own records, something that all the smart mutha-fuckas were doing. I changed the game for hip-hop, stretching its parameters, and now *I* was the laughingstock.

My reputation was more important than selling millions of albums. 50 had the Feds on my case. My music family was beginning to fall apart. And, my musical contributions were under attack. With my reputation being challenged, how was I supposed to get my shit back on track?

THERE HAD BEEN A LOT of backlash about the name Murder Inc. In an effort to calm things down, we took the "Murder" off of our name. I admit, to compensate, we used the word "murda" as much as we could in our joints. And based on what we were doing and what was in the media, it seemed like murder and violence were our sole activities. Truthfully, when I referenced "murda" in my joints, I was representing the label. It was like Diddy saying "bad boy" in all of his joints. The "Inc." never had the same impact. We had been cut at the knees. After Def Jam dropped us, we had to try to salvage what was left of the company.

I didn't have control over what was happening in my life—more accurately, control over what was happening to my career. I didn't know what to do. I just wanted to retaliate in some way. In response, I put out a full diss *album*, called *Blood in My Eye*. I took the name from a great book of the same name by George L. Jackson, a Black Panther who was murdered in prison at the hands of corrections officers. The book is famous for its brilliant analysis of the Black man's experience. Jackson was murdered. He was trying to escape. The story of George Jackson reminded me of Tupac, never having a chance to rise to his greatest self. Although *Blood in My Eye* was not my greatest-selling album, it remains a pivotal part of my whole body of work. Creatively and emotionally it did what it needed to do for me. Be that as it may, the album was too late to make its point. The avalanche had already started.

IT WAS NEW YEAR'S EVE 2003 and Aisha was pregnant with Jordan, my second son. The crew went to Las Vegas. I invited her along. Irv had gotten us a deal with Fox to do a hip-hop version of *New Year's Rockin' Eve*. We were trying to do a New Year's countdown that had some flavor.

We were all in a club a little away from the Strip, trying to chill and have a good time. The club had set up a roped-off VIP area for the crew and Aisha. I never liked VIP areas in clubs. I wanted to be near the people and let them meet me and speak with me. Aisha never liked that. "Jeffrey, you know people are crazy."

I convinced her to let us sit in another semi-VIP area that was closer to the dance floor and easier to be a part of the party. Once we got situated in the new booth, a random dude came up to me, pretending to be a fan. He small-talked me for a minute and then he just snatched the bottle that I was drinking out of my hand. "What the fuck are you doing, homie?" I asked.

Black saw the altercation and snuffed him. I clocked the dude with the bottle and then we all beat the shit out of him. I was enraged at the audacity of someone starting some shit with my pregnant wife sitting right there. I wanted to show him that he had disrespected me and my wife.

Arms and hands were flailing, girls were screaming, thugs were gathering around. Someone swept Aisha away from the scene and into the back of the club which had a private room for the owners. We left the club quickly. My clothes were covered in blood. I couldn't wait to get them off of me. We went back to the hotel. Aisha went right to the room to get the clothing away from us. I called one of my boys to come to my room and dispose of the clothes.

"Burn them," I said.

My security team took them in the plastic bag that hotels give you for your laundry.

Once the clothes had been burned, and we had all showered, it looked as though it never happened. I left Aisha to talk to my boys about what had just happened.

"Rule, we left that nigga for dead. That shit could come back to haunt us . . ."

"Who *was* that nigga? What the fuck just happened, man? Why would a muthafucka come up and do some shit like that to me?" I asked to no one in particular.

"Whatever it was, we took care of that shit."

I was disappointed that this had happened. A lot of these things that were happening I didn't want them to happen. I know I have a bad temper and the friends around me have bad tempers. This combination was volatile. It was creating situations that were becoming potentially dangerous. I wanted to get away from it. I just didn't know how. At some point, I was starting to understand what Jay-Z said, "Everybody that comes with you can't go with you."

When we got back home, my man Cici already knew the whole story. It had traveled fast to Los Angeles.

"Rule, the homies are in an uproar about what happened in Vegas. The nigga was in the *hospital*. You should do something for him, Ja. You guys beat him up pretty badly," Cici called to tell me.

"What the fuck do I have to do for *him*?" I screamed on Cici. "That nigga's the one who violated *me*! He grabbed *my* bottle out of *my* hand. Get the fuck outta here, Cici." I hung up on him.

MEANWHILE, A DETECTIVE came to Moms' front door. From outside the door, he said, "Mrs. Atkins, my name is Detective Smith and I have something important to talk to you about."

Moms didn't trust the police. She knew that they were always saying one thing in order to get to another. From inside the door, she said, "What's it about, officer?"

"There's a hit out on your son's life. Jeffrey Atkins, a.k.a., Ja Rule."

Moms slowly opened the door a little wider. She listened to what the detective was saying about California, Las Vegas and some gang activity. Moms had heard of the gang violence in California but didn't understand how I got involved in all of that being from New York. She listened a little longer then slammed the door. She was concerned but didn't tell me the police had came by until later, after another visit.

The detectives came back to see her two more times, trying to get inside the house, trying to see if I lived there. I had been in the Feds' files for a while now in relation to Murder Inc. and the drug money that supposedly funded the label. They were looking for anything that they could get on me, to take me down with Irv.

THE GUARD AT MOMS' GATED COMMUNITY told her later that the detective had said the guard didn't need to alert Moms anymore, that the guard should just open the gate. My Moms didn't like that. It was some more sneaky shit.

Moms hadn't trusted cops since the days of them harassing me on the corners and in the building. The cops had always been in our lives as far as I could remember. I have been ditching and dodging them my whole life, it seems. Moms always complained, "Police have a racial thing against rappers and ball players. They think y'all think that y'all are above the law."

"MAY WE COME IN?" the detective asked when he surprised my Moms by being at her front door for the second time.

"No, officer. There's no need for you to come in. We can just talk here. What do you need to know, now?"

"Is your son home?"

"No."

"When will he be back?"

"I don't know."

"Do you know where he is?"

"No, officer, I don't know. He is an adult."

"Thanks for your time," one detective said as the other one was peering over Moms' shoulders trying to catch a look at anything possibly suspicious that they could link to me.

Moms didn't want to upset me. She tried to keep these visits from me. When the detectives came for the third time, Moms had to tell me.

"Jeffrey, we need to talk."

"What's up, Ma?"

"The police came to see me today. There's a hit out on your life." As she spoke her voice started to tremble. My Moms is a crier.

"Why didn't you tell me? When did they come? What did they say?" I was starting to get angry at the thought that the police were involving my Moms with all this bullshit. She didn't do anything wrong.

"I didn't want to upset you," she said softly.

"How many times did they come?" I asked.

"Just once. . . . Twice. Well, three times," she stuttered.

"I'll take care of it. Don't worry. They won't be back," I said as I hung up the phone.

I called my lawyer immediately and the visits stopped.

But the fear and concern were still there. My daughter was almost four years old and there was a hit out for my life over a bullshit fight. I'm not even from the West Coast. I don't know anything about that shit. I didn't have the time or energy to fight anymore. The guy sued me and I ended up paying him $150,000 to squash it.

IRV SOUNDED WORSE than I'd ever heard him sound. "Nigga, you won't believe *this* shit." I was on the road at the time, still doing shows, despite the shit that was going on at home.

Irv continued, "The Feds came up to the office took our shit, computers, files and everything. Those muthafuckas are even freezing our accounts. They're shutting our shit down."

The Feds had put an indictment on Gotti and they were trying to investigate me as well, but there wasn't any evidence on me.

All of the hype of Murder Inc. was dead. And, it was all over *lies*.

DESPITE ALL OF THIS DRAMA, the show must go on: So I released my third album, *Pain Is Love*. And my fourth album, *The Last Temptation*, included the joint "Murder Reigns," which is all about the shit with the Feds.

It was a tough time for me. I think the hardest part of the whole mess was that I felt betrayed by my fans. All those years of being in the spotlight and having crowds approach me for autographs and photos, I never once said no. It really fucked me up that my fans turned on me like that. What people didn't understand was that the things that 50 Cent was saying about me, teasing me about singing and shit on my joints, he actually was singing, too . . . and making bigger records than before.

No one wanted to admit that the hard edge of rap and the melodies of R&B were a winning combination. It hurt because I really thought that my fans had genuine love for me. The same dudes that once were rooting for me were hating on me because 50 Cent said I sang on records. This whole thing made me really think about my life and the volatile hip-hop business. Popularity and fame are fleeting. That is the most important lesson that I have learned. I can't rely on fans to make me feel good about myself. The only person who can do that is *me*.

I've learned from all that I've been through that feeling good about yourself is based on your treatment of others. That's the measurement of our humanity.

EVERYBODY WANTED TO INTERVIEW ME about this beef shit. I agreed that I would only do one interview and the media could pull from that. We were thinking about who we could get like Barbara Walters or Oprah but in reality, this ghetto shit doesn't touch their world. We decided that we would go with Minister Louis Farrakhan. It sounded like a good idea at the time. Unbeknownst to us, the minister invited 50 Cent. Once again 50 was a no-show. I didn't care because I didn't want him there, anyway. I felt like the minister and I were having a conversation rather than an interview. He discussed a peace thing and a truce between young Black men. He explained that I had to think more broadly about the impact of two successful Black men publicly arguing. We talked about the power of bringing the community together, restoring the strength of Black men, maintaining our families and protecting the community. I have nothing but love and respect for him.

My nonsense felt weak in the face of his clarity. He had a vision for a whole race of people and I didn't even have a vision for my life. I mostly listened to him speak about Allah and the importance of not resorting to violence.

I was young. I wanted him to see my side of the whole thing. The minister said to me, "I love Ja Rule and I love 50 Cent."

I see now that he was there to tell me that I had to love myself. In doing so, I would be able to love 50 Cent. It would

also allow me to appreciate what me and 50 have done col-
lectively for hip-hop. Imitation is the greatest form of flattery.

OFF-CAMERA, THE MINISTER and I had some real talk. And
although he is who he is, he reminded me that even he has history with "beefs." He explained that he is no stranger to beefs.
In fact, he said something that I still think about to this day.
He said, "At one point in my life, even I had to choose between
my mentor and my leader. I chose my leader. So I know what
you're saying, my brother."

September 22, 2011

Today is Britt's Birthday. She's 16 today. I can't even begin to explain how fucked up I feel not being there for her on such an important B.Day. I feel empty, hollow as I write this. My thoughts are like echoes hitting the paper, they mean nothing. But as they bounce back they start to have meaning. She's still, and will always be, Daddy's lil BABY. Knowing that I've givin her everything a father could up until this point makes me feel proud. But yet so lost that I'm missing this milestone in her life. There'll be many more . . . graduation, college, marriage. I just never thought jail would be the reason I missed any of them. I spoke wit her today and she sounded happy. But I don't know if that made me feel better or worse. I was happy that she was in good spirits but sad I wasn't there to share that joy. I guess I can't be all things all the time even if all I wanted was just to be there. The funny thing is I probably won't be all that missed. I mean, shit, she is a teenager. LOL.

HAPPY BIRTHDAY BRITTNEY ASJA ATKINS 143
I LOVE YOU !

TEN

A Rock Star

THERE WAS JUST NO TIME FOR HATERS. I WAS IN LOS ANGELES recording my second album, *Rule: 3:36*. I thought it was one of the best times of my life. I rented a house and lived there for three months while I completed the album. I barely slept, as I was too busy enjoying the trappings of success. This was the first time that I had ever had anything extravagant like this. It was a beautiful home worth 10 to 15 million dollars. At first, we were staying at the hotel waiting for the house to be prepared for us. I was anxious. I didn't want to wait for the furniture and all of that stuff. I convinced my boys to get some blow-up mattresses. We went to Rent-a-Center and got some furniture and TVs. At the time, I didn't know that you couldn't have Rent-a-Center furniture in a place like that. There were beds and a couple couches and TVs everywhere. I had so many people staying there. It was like a revolving door.

There was one room we called the dorm room. It had about eight blow-up beds in there. If people didn't have a bedroom of their own, they had to stay in the dorm room.

I called the house my "ghetto mansion." It was located in Nichols Canyon, in the foothills of Los Angeles. I knew that I had arrived being where Julia Roberts, Ellen DeGeneres and Bruce Willis lived. I really wanted to be there. The house rented for $30,000 a month. I didn't have the slightest clue of what to do in a house like that. The house had eight bedrooms, nine bathrooms, a tennis court, a basketball court and a pool. Needless to say, I never played tennis, but we played hoops and hosted pool parties almost every day.

We had lots of fun in that house. At two or three in the morning we were playing basketball. You know how niggas play basketball, all loud. The police came up there nightly. Every time they came, I had a smart-ass remark for them.

"What you mean I can't have a party up here. I'm paying like everybody else." Don't be fucking with me. What you mean I can't have company." I am sure my neighbors hated us.

Sometimes in the mornings before anyone else was up, I would wander through the halls of the huge house, and as the blasts of sunlight touched my skin, I realized that I was experiencing my own version of the euphoria. I was light and carefree. I was free from the everyday shit. I was rich. Anything and everything I wanted was at my fingertips.

As I wandered through those hallways, I would remember Moms, who struggled to pay $700 a month for rent. I remember her negotiating with herself which bill to pay that month and which would be skipped. I looked at where I'd come from.

I had sacrificed a lot for everything that was happening to me. This was happiness.

I didn't quite understand the magnitude of what my life had turned into. My life had become a playground with all of my friends, old and new, being a part of my dream. This was my moment. I was tangled up in the web of being "Ja Rule." Somewhere in the back of my mind, I thought of Aisha and Brittney, but I kept telling myself that everything I was doing was for them.

As much as *Venni Vetti Vecci* was very personal, *Rule 3:36* was equally personal because it chronicled what was going on in my new life, real-time. "Between Me and You" was a sexy song about indiscretions between consenting adults. The record was a sign of what young men and women were going through—trying to cover up scandalous behavior. Irv and his wife, Deb, were going through it. Me and Ish were going through it. A few of my homies had gotten chicks pregnant on the West Coast. The song embraced a moment in time that we could never get back. We couldn't make up for it either. It was life. I like to make truthful records about what I see going on around me.

Los Angeles is a tough city to adjust to if you're not already rich and famous. There were lots of women around us at all times and I knew my boys wanted to meet some of them. Because I was the "star," it was very easy for me to meet women and pawn them off to my crew, who was always hungry for some female attention. There was this one particular girl who followed us from club to club. She was always watching and staring at me. She introduced herself and an innocent acquaintance started.

Some of the dudes in my circle got closer to her. From the brief conversation we had, I knew she was trouble. Every time I saw her she would name drop: "I am getting married to Fred Durst." "Tonight I'm going to visit Maxwell." "I am seeing Lenny Kravitz." Why did she need to tell us any of this? I knew she was lying or was a troublemaker. She had moved to Los Angeles looking for roles in music videos to get some exposure for her acting career.

I was shooting the video for "Between Me and You." When we arrived, Ezette was lying in the grass topless with a bikini bottom on. Everyone came to party, eat, hang out and do drugs that I was supplying. I wanted everyone to be able to say that if you are at Ja's house, you can have anything your heart desires.

This Ezette chick reminded me of the hoes from back in the day. Her sexual appetite was robust and she had no problem with having sex with as many men as she could in one night. All of the crew had their chance with Ezette. I called her a "throw around."

Our rental house was above the city and often had no signal for my cell phone. I never bothered to put in a home phone. Days went by without me calling home.

Aisha didn't know how to reach me. *What if something happened to Brittney?* I never thought of that shit, in those days. I was doing a combination of drugs. It was weed, alcohol and ecstacy. You never knew what you were getting with the X. It depends on what the X was cut with. It would give me a different high. I pride myself on never doing the hard drugs—coke, heroin—but the truth of the matter is that the X would be cut with all of that.

It seemed not a day went by that there wasn't another team of paparazzi following me around and taking photos of me and everyone around me.

All I could do was to endure the bullets of rage that Aisha was shooting every time she heard the sound of my voice. Aisha and I were fighting a lot. She'd scream at me. I'd hang up. She'd call back. I'd listen to her and then I'd hold on to all I had as an excuse: *work*. I gripped tightly to the rationalization that what I was doing was for our family. She threatened to leave me. I really didn't want her to go. She called me an asshole. I thought she was acting crazy. She told me that she hated me. I didn't say anything. I understood.

I was living a rock star life. I'll never forget the time I went to apply for life insurance. I called myself answering the questions truthfully. He asked me if I smoked or drank. I told it straight up. "Yeah, I smoke weed all the time and drink Henny every day. I don't think I'll live to be twenty-five." He thought I was crazy. I was.

The thing about life insurance is that one should be as healthy as possible to get the lowest rates possible. But I was thinking that it was like seeing a doctor, where you should be as truthful as possible to get an accurate diagnosis. In actuality, I should have lied to him and saved some money.

I was recording *Rule: 3:36* in the available hours between partying and losing my grip on reality. My boys were renting fast, expensive cars such as BMWs and Ferraris. Often under the influence, we would have accidents. But it was not always our fault. I remember one night me Gutta and H.O. were driving back to the house when a Jeep came out of nowhere. The tires were blown out. There were sparks flying from the rims scratching the concrete. He was on the wrong side of the road coming straight at us. I yelled for Gutta to get out the way. On the right side there were parked cars. On the left was oncoming traffic. Gutta tried to swerve, but we ended up crashing into the Jeep because we couldn't get out of the way. The crazy shit is that we would get into another car that was part of the convoy and we'd leave those cars right where we crashed them. The next day, I would just call my business manager and have her handle it—throwing money after bad decisions.

She always said the same thing, "Jeff you have to stop doing this!"

I must be an adrenaline junkie. That's what scares me about me. I've always been curious to see the other side. Maybe that's what keeps me strong. Fear goes out the window when you're drawn to the things that can get you killed. When those Jamaicans held a gun to my head, I wasn't scared. I just accepted the fact that that could have been my last day breathing. Since I was a kid, it's always been the same way. I seemed to be pulled by death, running towards it, gripping life's ragged edge, peering into the abyss, fantasizing about the other side.

I MADE TWO PHONE CALLS one night. I called my LA tattoo artist, Marc, and I called Moms.

"Jeff, what are you up to now?" Moms said laughing, finally hearing from me. It had been three weeks.

"Ma, how do you spell Kristen's name?"

"Kristen? Why?" she asked.

"How do you spell it?" I insisted.

"K-R-I-S-T-E-N," Moms spelled it out, carefully.

"Thanks, Moms. I'll hit you back when it's done." I hung up before she could ask anything else.

We used to go to the club and bring the club back to the house, since shit closed at two a.m. Gutta and BJ only had to mention it to two or three people in the club and the house would be crowded within an hour. It meant a lot to me to be able to host Los Angeles. I'm open to all kinds of people and loved having an eclectic group of celebrities, gangbangers, groupies, athletes, aspiring artists and hip-hop enthusiasts who were in the know.

I had a lot of love for LA because when my first album came out, LA is the city that gave "Holla Holla" a lot of love. I felt I owed the people in LA a good time. Our parties were always the place to be in Los Angeles.

The parties were round-the-clock affairs. At the house, we would swim, shoot hoops and drink freshly chilled champagne. Sometimes I would have Marc there, pay him a day rate of $5,000 and let him tattoo anyone who asked. Additionally, I would make sure that my drug guy was always there and fully equipped with his gray box, filled with every drug in existence.

THE CREW WENT OUT that night and was surprised when I said I wanted to stay home, alone. But that particular night, I couldn't face another crowd of scantily clad women and the scent of liquor on everyone's breath. I couldn't stand to see one more woman bring her child to the party, because she didn't have a babysitter.

I was really missing Kristen and who I imagined that she would have been to Moms and me. I wondered if Kristen could have kept our father from walking out on us. There were so many thoughts around that precious little girl. She should have lived. I was thinking hard about Kristen.

Nothing would take away the memory of Kristen; the sister I never knew. The little sister that I never got to walk to school, help with her homework or protect from l'il dudes who would have been scared of me.

Marc arrived just as the sun was setting. I led him into the huge white gourmet kitchen. The kitchen cabinets held an impressive inventory of Rémy Martin. The Sub-Zero refrigerator kept all of the vodka and Veuve Clicquot champagne perfectly chilled.

I had just gotten some work touched up by Marc a few days before and since then nothing had changed in the kitchen, except there were more fast food bags, plastic utensils and soiled Styrofoam containers spilling out of the garbage can. Marc headed towards the huge dining room table and started to prep. He went to the bathroom and took out several clean white towels. He disinfected the long table with a spray bottle and then covered the table with the towels. He had clamps to keep them in place. Next out of Marc's little doctor's bag came a small pillow for my head and chin to rest on. Without even looking, he placed a small blue box of alcohol pads on the table and last he carefully removed the colorful inks and laid them out one by one.

"No party tonight?" he asked.

"Nah, I took a break." I was slightly embarrassed.

"How did those touch-ups heal?" he asked.

"They're cool. I want to put the name 'Kristen' on my back with a halo on top and wings on either side. Here's a sketch that I did. I'm no artist, by the way."

"That's cool. I can see what you want," said Marc.

"Just give me something in a feminine script. I just want it large and real . . . beautiful, ya know. She would have liked that shit."

"Do you mind me asking who's Kristen? Is it your wife?"

"Nah. My baby sister."

Marc must have seen it in my eyes, there was nothing more to ask. He hesitated then pulled out his sketchpad and went to perfecting the sketch that I presented to him. After about twenty minutes, he handed the enlarged drawing to me for my final approval.

"That's it. That's it! It's dope, man." The tattoo was going to be a worthy memorial for Kristen. I had smoked a little weed before he got there. I didn't drink anything that day because when you are getting tattooed, drinking causes you to bleed more.

Zzzzzzzzzzzz sang the buzz of the needle as Marc powered it up. I drifted off to a psychedelic ink-filled dream while Marc raised the dead, tattooing all that was left of Kristen, so I could hold on to her, forever.

IT WAS AT THE L'ERMITAGE HOTEL in Los Angeles, a place that I used to go when the mansion got to be too much. I would sneak out, leaving the house in full-throttle party mode. The night I almost overdosed on fucking drugs, my boys' crew wanted to take me to the hospital. I told them, "No." I wasn't going to no hospital.

Even in that state, I was conscious enough to fear the media spotlight running away with how far down I'd fallen. I didn't want any more shit documented about me for my wife and daughter to ponder for the rest of their lives. I didn't want them to have to pump my stomach and put my autopsy results all over the Internet. I didn't want the world to be able to say that it was hip-hop's fault.

As my vision blurred, I remembered that I was still a strong-willed, strong-minded person. I knew that I'd gone too far. I was hurting my family, destroying my body and only I could do something about it. I knew I had to pull myself back from the edge for good.

WHEN I WROTE THE SONG "Put It on Me," I was thinking about Aisha and what we had been through and what we were going through. The only way I can say what I truly mean is through music. When we are yelling at each other through the phone, I know that she can't hear me. It seems like a song is the only way to get through to her. When I wrote "Put It on Me," I was hoping to get through.

Aisha was going through a lot of shit too. After a while when she couldn't get in touch with me, she just went into "fuck you" mode, which kept her strong. She stopped picking up her phone, too. Aisha isn't a crier.

There were a lot of issues of trust and fidelity or lack thereof. Everything had happened so fast. We'd gone from Aisha having to work a $10.25-an-hour job teaching mentally challenged kids how to comb their hair to moving into a huge house and having anything our hearts desired. And, as much as she enjoyed the new life and the recognition, it meant that I was no longer hers alone. I was public and everything *I* did was public—whether it was meant to be or not. Aisha was trying desperately to make sure that nothing or no one would threaten the relationship that we'd struggled so hard to keep. Now I can understand that shit.

It was like those paparazzi muthafuckas were tracking my every move. Every recording session, every party that we had, every bitch that came near me would be captured in a photo and all over the Internet within hours. As a result, Aisha and I had some lively arguments that sometimes ended up with her being violent. She has swung at me and I've had to hold her until she calmed the fuck down. She has hit me over my head with my cell phone and she has actually tried to take my head off of my body a few times. But, I was never violent with her. I understood. *I hurt her badly.* I still hadn't learned how to have my family and my art at the same time.

When I was in Miami for the Winter Music Conference, we were just about to drop another album. Since Murder Inc. had always been supported by radio, Gotti and I came up with a brilliant idea for a gift for the programming directors. We hadn't spoken to Ezette from LA in a while, but when Irv suggested we have her as the gift for the PDs we thought it was a good idea. And it was.

When she was called, she was surprised.

"Do you want to come to Miami? We got some money for you," said one of my crew.

"Who'll be with you?" she asked.

"The usual suspects, all of the niggas you know."

"Okay, I'll come."

Irv and I knew it was an evil plan but it made sense. The PDs at the conference would be mostly overweight, balding, middle-aged men who hadn't been laid in months, maybe years. Ezette was the perfect gift. She was happy to oblige. We got her a hotel room with a view. When we got to the conference, we told all the radio guys that we needed that there was a gift waiting for them in Room 3261.

The radio guys flew to the room and Ezette gave them each the time of their lives. And of course, Murder Inc. would have another amazing year at radio.

When dropped at the airport, Ezette was grateful for the generous tip that she got.

"My real name is Karinne."

This is part of the game—never delivering. To be hugely successful in entertainment, people have to want to fuck you. Women have to want to fuck you and men have to want to be like you. Think about Michael Jackson and Prince. They're enigmas that never delivered on the dream. Here's the dream for fans. I'm at a concert. I love Prince. I can see him, but I can't touch him. I can't talk to him. I can't get to him. This is an example of never delivering. So, the person goes to concert after concert, trying to get closer and closer. This never delivering on the dream made the business go. It made fans come back for more and more. When Usher made his first album, he was a single guy and women adored him. When he got married, his fans' dream of sleeping with him was shattered. I believe this was reflected in the sales of the albums as a result. See, the biggest stars never deliver. They are the dream. But it has all changed drastically now with social media. Now fans feel like they know you. We get to speak on Twitter. Being more accessible lowers a performer's value.

I'LL NEVER FORGET the time Aisha and Dennis and I were in the Range Rover going into the city. We were in the narrow-ass Lincoln Tunnel. Aisha said something that I don't even remember, but I'm almost sure it had to do with women or the fact that I was away or going away again soon. She might have said something about the video I was going to make next week or the interview that was on the newsstands where I had insinuated that I was available. She cringed every time she saw me in a video, sexing up another woman for the whole world to see. "Why did you have to touch her butt like that?"

This time, I snapped. I started swerving the car from lane to lane, recklessly. It was my way of saying that I had had it. That I didn't want to have that conversation again. I was screaming, "I'll kill us all!" I was out of control. I was angry at myself for who I had been to Aisha over the last few years. I was angry at myself for driving her crazy. I was angry at life for being so complicated.

At that moment, perhaps it would have been better if we had hit something to stop the lunacy that had gotten us to that point in the Lincoln Tunnel. Aisha was frustrated, too, but she wasn't afraid.

When I look back on that night, I think I could have killed us. I could have hit the wall or another car filled with innocent lives. I could have killed someone else's family as I swerved in and out of my own problems. God always looks out for children and fools and that is what I was.

PART THREE

Pain Is Love

*

April 6, 2012

Today is Jordan's Birthday and I'm happy I was able to call home to tell him I love him and wish him one. He turns 9 today, my youngest and most pleasant child, HA HA. He doesn't really understand all this jail bullshit and it's hard to explain to him why I can't be there for his Birthday and even harder to explain if I wasn't able to call due to this fucking slug I just caught. Luckily they didn't serve me yet so I was able to hear his happy lil voice. AAAHHHH such joy the little things bring when you're in prison. The things I often took for granted—I missed so many Birthdays and Holidays when I was home on the road doing shows. I used to think that was more important to make money so they can have nice things for their birthdays instead of being there for their birthdays. I guess that comes from me growing up not celebrating birthdays. To me it was just another day. But it's not so much about the birthday, as it is about spending quality time with my kids. Somewhere along the way I guess I missed that point. Lucky for me that by this time next year I'll be home for Jordan's 10th and I'm not just talking home from prison, I'll be home with my son.

HAPPY BIRTHDAY . . . JORDAN NILE ATKINS
I LOVE YOU!!!

*

ELEVEN

My Father

WHEN MY COUSIN COREY CALLED TO INVITE ME TO DINNER AT his parents' house, the idea of a home-cooked meal with Aunt Dell and Uncle Walter sounded like just what I needed after the tornado of shit that I'd been through. Corey heard about my sold-out show in Miami, and hoped that I could make time for a Sunday dinner. Moms always said that I should stay in touch with my father's family, although it got harder and harder for her to stay close to them. It was rough on Moms because of what had happened between them.

I did stay in touch, but not every day. When I moved from always-in-trouble to famous, I became the golden child of the family. Rather than hold anything against my family, mother's side or father's side, I always tried to take the high road. I've always considered family the most important thing in life. I was never spiteful when my family disfellowshipped my mother. I didn't hold it against them and I continue to let stuff roll off my back. I don't bring up old wounds. When someone in my family has a financial crisis, of course they call me first. I don't feel burdened by it because I know they only call if they really need it. They definitely don't take advantage. I have never forgotten the struggles I went through growing up, so I recognize that people need from time to time. Being accomplished makes it my responsibility to help to make each generation stronger in my family. White households have generations of successful people. As Black people we're working on that still.

When I accepted the invitation, Corey said something that I wasn't expecting. "Oh yeah, your father will be there."

I had been thinking about my father a lot and wanted to reestablish a relationship with him. I'd heard that he was thinking about me, too. My father was always in me, even when he wasn't with me. Like him, I mistakenly thought that drugs and alcohol would be able to slow my life down because it always felt like being in a speeding car without a seatbelt on. Instead of slowing things down, drugs accelerated everything, sending my life spinning out of control. Although drugs seem to temporarily calm you, when reality hits, it hits hard, shattering everything that ever mattered.

That Sunday, Aunt Dell and Uncle Walter's small brick ranch house was packed with my father's family, who I hadn't seen in over a decade. Everyone was there, Cousin Corey, my Uncles Gary and Glenn and my Aunts Marie, Brenda and Cathy were all there. I was sorry that Moms wasn't there. She had been so close to Aunt Brenda back in the day when they all lived in Queens and Aunt Brenda worked at the same hospital that Moms worked at. The house was full of family and smells of good food that triggered warm memories of my past.

The last time I had seen my dad was in Florida, where my grandparents eventually moved. I was about sixteen and my Moms took me. My father was at the house and after all those years, my parents were right back where they started. Moms was getting mad and my father was ready to get physical, which is all he knew how to do. He asked Moms to go into a room so that they could discuss the issue without me.

"I'm not going to leave you in the room alone with my Moms."

"Son, this is not your fight, please get out of the way," he said as if he thought he had a place in our family. As if he had a say about me or her.

I didn't know what else to do, so I jumped on him, took his head in my arms and put him in a headlock. My father was taken aback when I grabbed him. He was breathing heavily and threw me against the wall. I headed towards him again, like a bull, until my paternal grandfather came into the room and pulled us off of each other. Moms was crying in the corner.

"Jeff! Let's go. Let's go. I can't take this!" And we left.

Although I had accepted the invitation, I realized that I was completely unprepared to deal with him and all the years of pain and anguish that he had caused me. I had buried the pain so deeply, hoping that it would never resurface.

He stepped towards me and said, "I've missed you, son." My feelings of abandonment, being alone and unloved, were all jumbled up in my heart. Throughout my life, each violent blow that I'd dealt held a little piece of him. Not knowing what else to say or do, I embraced him like a young Black man caught off guard, but who had finally found what he was looking for. Plus, offering a hug is my normal way.

MY FATHER AND I awkwardly "kicked it" at first, both of us commenting on how much we had both changed and how good it was to see each other. My father was awkward. His body moved slowly and he was no longer in good shape. He had fattened up. His face was different but I couldn't pinpoint what it was. His face was fuller and less handsome.

He gently patted my back as if to confirm, for himself, that I was real. My mind raced trying to find the right words to say to him, but I couldn't get them out of my mouth. Uncle Walter watched the two of us from the corner of his eye. When he realized that we needed some privacy, he put his hand on my back and led me and my father to the back bathroom.

"Y'all can sit in here, it's not so noisy," Uncle Walter said with a slight Southern drawl as he started to close the door on us.

"Thanks, Uncle Walter," I said as the door shut.

My father sat down on the commode. "Say what you need to say. I'm ready."

I sat down uncomfortably on the edge of the large bathtub. I detected that although he was supposed to be clean, he may not have been. I sat across from him, trying to collect my thoughts. We both studied the tiny cracks in the tile.

My heart raced and my skin tightened as I was able to muster, "You've missed a lot."

"I know, son, and I'm sorry for that." His hair was graying and his skin was a similar dull shade. Although the years had formed an intricate gap between us, he seemed comfortable with me, as if we were once connected in another life.

"I have a wife and two children now. My wife's name is Aisha and Brittney is my daughter. She's eight. Jeffrey Jr. is my son. I call him L'il Rule. He's three."

"Wow! Man. That's real cool. I hope to meet them someday. I hope to be a better grandfather than I was a father," he said, hoping that it wouldn't be too late. He sat up a little taller and said, "I'm *real* proud of you, son."

"I've been through a lot," I said. "A lot of the shit I've been through has to do with you, I think. I forgive you, man, for most of that shit, but what I can't forgive is you hitting my Moms and walking out on me. You *can't* leave your kids."

"Jeffrey, it's so hard to explain. Sometimes I don't understand it, either. I was so fucked-up on drugs. I didn't know if I was coming or going. I wasn't myself. My next hit was all I cared about. I hurt anything that was standing in my way. It didn't matter who it was, what it was or how hard I hit."

"I don't need you to explain. You think I don't know about that shit?" I could feel myself getting mad.

"Too bad you don't remember your grandfather. He was like a wild cowboy, himself," my father said, smiling at the memory. It was nice to see him crack a smile. My father's smile was familiar and I was able to feel what I felt back then, when I thought he was going to be my father.

"Jeff, you know my father wasn't there for me, either," he said somberly. "I know how you feel. It's a shame that I followed in his footsteps as much as I planned to never do to you what he did for me. Life takes you by surprise," he said, shaking his head.

His mouth still formed that same smile that I loved as a child. Listening to him speak about his own father showed me that for all of us, our fathers are often our reason for being or our *excuse* for not being.

"You know, it's *cool* to be a father. It's the greatest reward you can have as a man. To raise your children to teach them to be respectable," I said.

As I sat across from him, I could feel the anger draining out of my heart. I didn't have to be mad anymore, because I had survived. There would never be enough time to deal with it all in one night, there was so much and so little to say.

But, I said nothing. The inimitable silence between estranged family members filled the space. It was drowning us in silence.

The bright lights of the bathroom allowed me to really see the sadness that lived in his eyes. I could see up close what drug addiction had done. I could see that as much as he may have wanted to do right by me, he *couldn't*. Drugs had eaten him up. His weathered face told the story that I knew all too well.

Strangely, seeing him again made me understand him better than I wanted to. I could finally see the two sides of the story. I could finally *forgive*.

"Son, I've waited years to be able to sit down with you and apologize. I often wondered what I would say to you. I just want to tell you that I am so proud that you are a family man, taking care of your children and your wife."

"I love them. I couldn't do anything else," I said.

"You're a good man, son. You're a better man than I was. I sit here and look at you and you know what fucks me up the most?"

"What?"

"That you had to do it all by yourself."

"It wasn't easy. But it wasn't impossible."

"Keep doing what you're doing, son. The world needs to see more examples of men being fathers and husbands."

"I hope that I will be able to tell my son Jeffrey that he is a better man than me, someday."

"That's *it*. That's how we break the cycle. One father at a time."

My father cleared his throat. "Son, I want to give you some advice."

I stopped him in his tracks. "With all due respect, pops, I made it this far. I think I'm good."

"I understand." He said it *again* after all those years.

His gaze revealed a father's greatest secret: that no man is ever ready for the weight of fatherhood. My own children taught me that a father has to do *one* thing, which is stay. The children will do the rest.

There was a knock at the door. It was Aunt Dell.

"Come in," we both said in unison.

Aunt Dell was flustered. Her apron was soiled with flour.

She smelled of melting cheese. "Dinner's ready, you two. Now it's time to eat. Jeffrey, I made your favorites."

"Okay, Aunt Dell. We'll be right out."

"Don't take too long, the cornbread is hot."

I looked at my father and heard myself saying, "Can I call you sometime?"

"I'd like that," he said. "I'll give you my number."

I pulled out my phone and punched in the numbers carefully as if my life depended on it. Once I got the numbers in, I didn't know how to label it. I hesitated and then my fingers typed the letters "D-A-D" and I pressed SAVE. Having a father acknowledge me, and become a part of my life, was validation. It increased my self-confidence right there on the spot.

I felt an overwhelming shudder of relief shooting through my whole body. I wished I could have left out of the back door to unravel these feelings instead of going out there to make small talk with a family that I had lost in the shuffle of life.

My father came over to me and gave me a long hug that I'll never forget.

I said, "I'll call you sometime."

"Jeff, I know how busy you are with your work. I'll understand if you can't find the time," he said, ironically preparing himself for abandonment. "Just know that you'll always be my son. And that you *do* have a father. Human relationships come in all shapes and sizes. This is just ours—it's no better or worse than anyone else's. Remember that."

"I will, Dad."

"You're living your dream. Most people can't say that about their lives. That's real good, son."

"What was your dream?"

"To open a bakery."

I wished I had known, but it was probably too late, I thought.

My father was an accomplished baker. He baked for the Queen of England. Rumor has it, according to my relatives, my father invented fat-free cheesecake.

"I want to come see your kids. My grandkids. Would that be all right?" he asked.

"Yeah, man. They'd like that."

"Now let's eat before Aunt Dell gets mad."

When we walked to the table the whole family was looking at us and smiling like Cheshire cats. No one said anything about what had happened. We tried to act as normal as we could, although a lifetime of pain had been lifted between the two Jeffreys that sat at the table.

My family wanted to talk about having someone famous in the family. "What is R. Kelly like?" "I heard you met Minister Farrakhan." "I don't like that 50 Cents!" I listened with half attention. I couldn't take my eyes off my dad. As I watched, I noticed how much I looked like him. How we held our fork the same. I noticed how quickly we ate, as though we were both racing against time. I was amazed at how funny he was. Moms always said he was a funny dude and Aisha says that about me.

I don't care what nobody says, young men *always* want to love their father. I realized then that I'd always loved mine. I'd always wanted him in my life. A boy's father is the only person who can hold his son accountable for his actions.

I kept my promise to him. I called him from time to time for the next few years. We were slowly building a rapport that made me feel whole. Mostly, we spoke about news, sports and music a little bit. I was surprised that he knew so much about hip-hop. I never talked about his leaving again. I didn't want to bring up old wounds.

The years seemed to fly by, speckled only with my occasional calls to see how he was doing. In 2008, he told me that he was having some health problems and he was scheduled to go into the hospital.

The whirlwind of my life was pulling me in so many different directions. I planned to go visit him in the hospital. I wanted to and until I got there, I called him almost every day.

The last time that I spoke to him he said, "Son, you have a sister in Queens."

I didn't know what to feel but I said, "That's great. How old is she?"

"She's about your age," he whispered.

I didn't want to react. I didn't want to remember the pain that my father's womanizing had caused Moms.

"You should go see her sometimes. She has a son, too. You are an uncle."

I wasn't sure about that. It would hurt Moms if I got involved with the child that my father had when he was married to her. Married to us.

"Yeah. I'll try," I finally said.

My Cousin Corey called to tell me that my father had passed away. I regretted that I never got to Florida in time to see him one last time. I was saddened by my loss and angry at the speed at which time flies.

I thanked Corey for letting me know and got off the phone with him, quickly. I didn't want to believe it. I called my father's number one more time with speed dial. The phone rang and rang and rang.

The least I could do was give my father a place to stay—with me. If I couldn't have him in life at least I could have him in death. His ashes rest in my home office.

*

July 26, 2012

*Well, here I am sitting in my 4x10 cell, just a few days over a year
to the day that I arrived at Midstate. I'm hot, with my little fan
that's blowing just enough air to keep me breathing in this mother
fucker. As I listen to my Walkman while the radio is playing
a throwback of the Fugees "No Woman No Cry" through my
headphones that I made into speakers. What a life. Thank God
this shit is almost over. It's been a Hell of a ride. But I'm looking
forward to getting off this train. Next Stop Home. It hasn't been
all bad, though. You'd be surprised how much you can grow in a
year. I've learned a lot about who I am and who the people around
me are. I've always thought about what it would feel like to see my
life from the outside looking in and I guess I'm getting that chance
except I'm actually getting a glimpse from the inside looking out.
What I've seen is not the person I envisioned. I use to think only
I knew what was best for me but I've put myself in situations I
wouldn't allow my worst enemies to be in. So does that make me
my own worst enemy? From where I'm sitting writing this right
now, I would assume so.*

*

TWELVE

My Wife

FAME GIVES YOU AN UNREALISTIC VIEW OF YOURSELF AND the world. I admit, sometimes, I took my fame too far. When you're famous, everyone caters to your every need and want. Everything is done the way you want it without exception. It can give you a crazy way of thinking and seeing things, mostly yourself.

Everything was incredible during this period. I was winning awards and traveling all around the world. I was able to buy my family homes. I was proud to tell my Moms that she could quit her job. In 2002 I won a BET Award for Best Male Artist and an MTV Award for "I'm Real" with J-Lo. Everyone was calling me to write songs for them. Labels were restripping albums to add a song written by me. Artists like J-Lo, Mary J, Enrique Iglesias and even Fat Joe. I was the first rap artist to be asked to write records for R&B and pop artists. At the time,

I didn't understand what it meant to be nominated for any of those awards. My dream was to go gold. I never thought or knew about what it would mean to have a number one record. Today, I look at an artist like Jay-Z and his first number 1 record was "Empire State of Mind." This let me know how big it was to hold that spot. There aren't many rap artists to hold the number one spot. I was even number one in the UK. These kinds of accolades were for pop artists, not rappers. When I was number one, I was ahead of artists like Britney Spears. On an occasion, I had either three or four records in the top ten at one time. That hadn't been done since the Beatles.

I think Big said it best: More money, more problems. I remember the minute that Aisha told me what happened. My DJ, DJ Daison, was hanging out with all of us. Aisha was with her girls at the night club. Daison was hanging out with them and he must have noticed that Aisha had an American Express Black Card in her wallet. He lifted it.

Ish realized right away that the card was gone and called the accountant. When we went to cancel the card we noticed some unauthorized purchases showing up from an online company that sold DJ equipment. Once I spoke to American Express, it all became clear. Someone named Daison Floyd was purchasing the DJ equipment.

We were on the road. I didn't say anything about it until the time was right. I was enraged, but kept my cool. I asked the tour bus driver to make a stop, with one thing only fixed in my head. I had always lived by the principle of an eye for an eye. If you steal something you should get your hands cut off. This is how life should be. If you rape someone you should be castrated. I feel if those things were implemented into society, we wouldn't have all of the troubles that we have with crime.

Like I said, I never liked sneak-shit-type crimes. We were on the road. I had the driver stop at a hardware store so I could get some tight gloves and a baseball bat. No one knew what was going on, but since it was my show and I said let's stop at the store, there were no questions.

I waited until later that night in the hotel. We were in Sacramento, California, and I had a beautiful suite with a big glass window looking out over the city. All I could think was I should whack Daison's head off right there. I reconsidered because by doing it near the window, I might break the glass and that wouldn't be good. I went into the bedroom of the suite. Everyone else was in the living room. I summoned Daison to come into the room so we could go over the show one more time. I had my gloves on, which sometimes I wore on stage. I had the bat in my hands and Daison didn't question it. All I remember is that I blacked out as soon as I started hitting him with that bat. I could hear the bitch whining, "What the fuck are you doing?" After a few more hits, he was able to run out of the room. I could see the look on his face. He thought I was going to kill him. He probably saw a blank stare from me. He didn't recognize me. I had turned into a different guy.

Everyone saw me coming out of the room behind him with the bat in my hand. Daison was holding his head, which was bleeding. I screamed, "Yo, Life, step on that nigga's arm!" And he did. When I got over there, I was hitting him with that bat so hard that I couldn't even stop. Even my boys were saying, "Rule, you've done enough. You proved your point. You're gonna kill him, Ja." My mind was in a different place. I could hear them but my hands couldn't stop. Someone had to stop me. Later my homies told me that I was yelling at him. "I had love for you, nigga! I brought you into the circle. I fed your family, nigga! You betrayed me!"

Daison didn't seem to understand that I was giving him a chance when muthafuckas wasn't even feeling him. It was like a straight slap in the face. They were callin' him a pretty boy and shit. They thought he was weak on the turntables. I had always been good to him. I was paying him $1,500 dollars a show. I had over forty shows booked that year. That's $60,000 plus all meals and accommodations *paid*. I wasn't a regular selfish type. I never treated my people differently than I treated myself. If I was staying in the Ritz-Carlton everyone was staying in the Ritz-Carlton. But, if someone does something foul to me, they get what they deserve. I could have beat Daison with my hands. I wanted to break his bones. *I wanted him to bear the weight of what he did by stealing from my wife.*

I really wanted him to know what he did was wrong and sit with that while he was in the hospital. He needed to know that he *fucked up*. I also did it as a message to the others. If another muthafucka in the crew was thinking of crossing me, they would think about it twice. We settled out of court. Daison sued me for assault. I paid him $80,000. I never spoke to him again.

I don't like to get mad at people. It takes up way too much energy that could be used creating music. I hated turning into my father.

ON APRIL 6, 2003, I almost passed out in the fucking hospital. I had never experienced such a feeling in my life. It was a take-my-breath-away, head-spinning, sweat-pouring, blurry-eyed *anxiety attack*. It was a frightening sensation. It took over my whole body. It felt like a tsunami had lodged inside of me, pushing me over from the inside. I was at the hospital waiting for my third child, Jordan, to be born.

"The umbilical cord is wrapped around the baby's neck," the doctor said to me.

There's a chance that my new baby boy may not live. But, God was listening. I wouldn't have been able to live if Jordan didn't make it.

But he did.

Jordan, as Jeffrey Jr. did, will grow up a wealthy kid with everything at his disposal.

I RECORDED *R.U.L.E.* UNDER THE INC. LABEL, AND IT WAS released in 2004. The joint was still hot no matter what the hip-hop heads were saying. The joint "Wonderful" with R. Kelly was hot and talked about all the fake-ass bitches that I'd met. It went number one in the UK, which never happens for American artists. The other hot joints were "R.U.L.E," "Never Thought" and "Life Goes On"—all *hot* joints. "What's My Name?" was a club anthem, and "New York" was strictly for my New York fans.

DURING THIS PERIOD, I was at the height of my career, but the music game was dragging me down. I felt the stress that I had felt when I was hustling on the corner. Now, instead of pushing drugs, I was pushing *hits*. It's the same hustle. You have to get your music to the fiends, the audience and the DJs are like the lieutenants stirring up the sales, getting radio interested in your shit. You have to make sure that the DJs that have your music are the ones with the right connects. It can't just be any DJ. Most of all you have to be out there, visible, showing the world that you are keeping it real. I had to remain strong and aggressive at all times. I really had to *hustle* to have a hit record and then I had to battle to keep it.

There were more run-ins with the law. My patience with bullshit was wearing thin. Everything and everyone in sight irritated me. In 2004, I was arrested for punching a man in a club in Toronto, Canada. All the way in Canada it was more shit having to do with 50 Cent. Don't get me wrong. These were not fights because someone was simply listening to 50 Cent or wearing a G-Unit T-shirt. These were matters of being disrespected. The guy in Canada said something to irritate me. He said into my ear, "G-Unit." It was an impulse reaction because he was just too physically close to me. That was the reason I punched him in his face. It was totally unnecessary. The case was all over the newspapers in Canada and the US. I *hated* putting Aisha and the kids through all of this stuff.

In 2005, I was arrested for driving with a suspended license and possession of marijuana. The walls of fame had come tumbling down.

A couple more people had gotten killed in Detroit, linked to Eminem's Shady Records. Now that Shady Records and Aftermath Entertainment were involved with 50 Cent, the fans in Detroit were a part of the beef. Eminem saw that he and 50 Cent were taking on each other's beefs and getting people killed who had no real affiliation with them. I even talked to MTV about it and I said the beef thing was wack. I told them that I was done with it. I hated being in trouble with the law. It just didn't look good to my kids.

IT WAS AROUND THIS TIME Aisha called me screaming on the phone. She was screaming so loudly that I had to excuse myself from the meeting that I was in. She screamed so loudly that she was losing her voice. I slid into an empty conference room and let her get it all out. I thought something had happened to one of the kids. My heart was racing so hard that I couldn't breathe. Finally, she shrieked, "I heard it on the radio. Don't deny it. Don't deny it, muthafucka!"

I had no idea what she was talking about.

"Do you know a bitch named Karinne? Because this is what she said about you *'Ja entered my body and I felt both pain and love simultaneously.'*" Aisha said angrily.

"I don't think I know her. Who is that bitch? Where would I know her from?" I said carefully.

"You may not know her but you certainly fucked her! Five days you were fucking her which is why you never answered your phone in California!"

"What?" My heart sank. "Babe, let me call you back. Someone just came in the room. I will call you right back. Stay calm. I love you." I said as I pushed END.

Karinne had written a book, and I had to get my hands

on it to manage this shit. Aisha knew everything already and I had to catch up.

I CALLED IRV. "Find out about Karinne. She wrote a book and I'm in it. Find it. Find it!"

They were talking about the book *Confessions of a Video Vixen* on every urban radio station across the country. Karinne Steffans wrote about all of her exploits with people in hip-hop that she'd fucked. There was a chapter in the book called "Pain Is Love." There was nowhere to hide.

Fame is the most dangerous drug of them all. Who would do that? Why would a single mother embarrass herself in order to make a little money and a lot of *unfortunate* fame? It's clever though, how she turned it into a franchise. But, today, nobody wants anything to do with her. One has to be careful about what they build their fame on. Snitching and hoeing are a weak foundation.

I thought that Aisha had already read each page over and over again, ingesting each word, ready to spit them back at me, but she hadn't. I didn't know what to do or where to go. I'd told Aisha that I'd call her back, but for the first time in my whole fucking life, *I was scared.* I didn't think I could take any more, with the police trouble, the media reports and now Aisha policing me more than ever.

BLACK HAD SURVIVED PRISON and I'd blown up. He was released during *Rule 3:36*. The year 2003 was the perfect time to do the Cash Money Click album with Black and O. I still wanted to do something good. It was important to me that I kept my promise to Black and O.

I went to Lyor and he gave me a verbal go-ahead to go over to TVT and do it. We recorded a full album that was dope. When it was almost finished, Lyor pulled the plug on us. He said simply, "Ja, you're not doing that." It became a new fight.

Steve Gottlieb of TVT proceeded to sue Def Jam for $100 million. Def Jam told Lyor that he would be responsible if Def Jam lost the case. For the first time, Lyor wasn't straightforward with me. He gave me a test and I failed it. He just wanted to see what I would do if I told him that I would record for Steve after all that Lyor and I had been through. Because I was thinking of my boys and not the business, I thought it would be cool. When he told me that I could do it, he was testing my loyalty. I failed. He pulled the plug. It wouldn't make good sense to "lend" me to Steve Gottlieb. I was one of Def Jam's top-selling artists.

Lyor felt that I should've been wise enough to tell Black and O that we weren't going to be able to do it. Cash Money Click was good, it just got fucked-up beyond our control. Making that album with them was the right thing to do. We called it *CMC EST 1995*, Cash Money Click, established in 1995. The album was hot. However, it was *never* released and there are no traces of it, anywhere.

In my situation, I could understand how slaves must have felt when white men were fighting over the fruits they had the potential to gain over the slaves' labor. It was about power, which is what white men need to live. All I wanted to do was keep my promise to my fans. Now I recognize the importance of keeping the big picture in view.

The lawsuit definitely strained my relationship with Lyor. Eventually, I did show my loyalty to Lyor in court, and Def Jam won the case.

Looking back, the whole thing a pissing contest between Lyor Cohen and Steve Gottlieb. They needed to show whose dick was bigger. That's how the corporate boys fight—in court.

*

August 1, 2012

Damn, time flies when you're having fun, HA. I'm almost done with this bullshit, 5 months and 20 days to the door. Can't wait to tell these punk ass COs to kiss my ass. At least I can say I accomplished a few things while I was here. For 1 I got my mother fuckin weight up. I came in like 160 and right now I'm 185 all muscle. It wasn't easy but I'm happy I put in the work. A lot of niggas came in and get fat. I wouldn't be able to look at myself if I did that. I haven't drank, smoked or fucked in almost 2 years. Shit I might be able to walk on water right now, LOL. At 36 I am in the best shape of my life. I also got my GED, finally. I thought it would make me feel good to get my diploma but it made me feel like an asshole that I didn't have one already. It didn't make me feel stupid 'cause I still had to study, take the test and pass. But it did make me realize just how many young Black men don't have High School Diplomas. They say that the average education in prison is 8th grade. That means the average man in prison is not even capable of passing the test. Case in point, when I took the pretest there was at least 30 guys who took it with me, but only 5 of them that actually passed and was able to take the GED. What's crazy is a lot of these young dudes look up to me and aspire to have some of the things that I've acquired in my life. But here I am in the same place as them taking the same fucking test. So what that I passed. Does it make me any smarter? Any better? To be honest I'm probably the dumbest nigga in the room 'cause I should be setting a better example, not only for them, but for my sons and my daughter. It's funny how prison has a way of solving that age old mystery of the tale of three stories . . . the one you're telling, the one they're telling, AND THE TRUTH!

*

THIRTEEN

The Mirror

THE PROBLEM WITH BEING FAMOUS IS THAT THERE ARE TOO many strings attached. Fans want you to do the things that you've always done over and over again. That's also what the labels want. Hip-hop doesn't like change.

Funny thing is that I never strived to be famous as much as I wanted to be *creative*. I really couldn't fathom the power that art could have over people until I was clocking chart-topping records and winning awards.

I YEARNED TO DO a more artistic and far-reaching album. I had recorded a set of new songs that were a surprising departure from my usual stuff. I called it *The Mirror* and presented it to Motown. The songs from *The Mirror* didn't have a lot of guest performers on it because I wanted it to be about me and what

I'd been through and how it changed me. I called it *The Mir-ror* because when you're standing in front of a mirror, all you see is you. Of course, the first singles weren't well received by radio, because they were different than they were accustomed to hearing from me.

Eventually, I ended up virtually giving the *The Mirror* away as a free download. I was no longer worried about the money, I just wanted to do something creative and give my die-hard fans a gift, after all we'd been through. *The Mirror* was ambitious but it was surprisingly well received by those who got it. People had tripped that I had R&B singers on my songs before. This time, I was the one who was singing! I took chances without being worried about the fans' reception, reviews or the record sales. I started *The Mirror* with a Gregorian chant. On the track "Father Forgive Me," I sampled the Beatles' classic hit "Eleanor Rigby," over which I sang the chorus. On "The Mirror," I reflected on my life, and on "Sing a Prayer 4 Me," I prayed for strength. I must admit that there were some hot street songs, too, like "Enemy of the State" and "Sunset," but overall there was a slightly different feel to the album, a certain new awareness. It showed that I'd been through some things and was becoming wiser than I had ever been. Wise enough to know that art was all that mattered.

This album proved to me that I am indeed an artist. I drew on everything, including travel, to put this album together. I had traveled a lot over the years. I had been to Europe and the Middle East; I even went to the Brazilian favelas and a war zone, in Kuwait, to perform for the 2001 USO tour with J. Lo and Kid Rock. I was able to bring Aisha to the USO tour in

Iraq in 2009. We both learned a lot about the world, just by standing on foreign soil. On one occasion, we stayed in one of Saddam Hussein's hunting lodges, where everything in the place was gilded in gold and silver.

I heard and saw everything around me in a new way. Middle Eastern music layered its sounds differently than what I was used to. I was really feeling their unique vocal styles, exotic instruments and language. Sensuality and spirituality rang out in every note. Just by hearing it, my music would never be the same again.

It's amazing what exposure does to a closed mind. When you travel and see different parts of the world, your eyes are opened to a whole new way of seeing. Leaving America showed me that people all over the world love hip-hop because there are so many more poor people in the world than rich. Hip-hop is the universal sound of oppression.

I couldn't understand what the international music was saying but it sounded *fresh*. We couldn't imitate it, but we *felt* it. That's what art does. It forces us to connect the dots between our inside and the outside.

ONE OF THE MOST ENLIGHTENING EXPERIENCES I had was performing at the favelas in Brazil with Fat Joe in 2008. When we accepted the show, to be honest, I didn't know what I was getting myself into. For me, it was just another show in an "unsavory" neighborhood. It didn't seem dangerous to me until I told people that I was going and all they could do was warn me about how dangerous it was.

These Brazilian favelas sat on a hill high above Rio de Janeiro. The favelas are totally unpoliced ghettos. *Everyone* is armed. There are no formal police because even they felt that it was too dangerous to go up there. Even the hardcore rappers in America declined the invitation. Only a rare few artists have taken the trip. I was the first in the hip-hop community. The only others to have made this trip are Madonna, Michael Jackson and Mos Def.

The sweeping views of the city below would never suggest the poverty, the danger and the anarchy that exist in this secluded area. In the favelas the crowded streets are lined with people of all ages who contribute to the system in one of four industries: cocaine, heroin, guns or human trafficking. It's a community where those things are the mainstay of the economy, because those are the things we do when we have no education.

The people are living in crumbling shantytowns, barely habitable, their homes held up only by shoddy sheets of aluminum that only cover the roof or patch up holes in the walls. They can't afford both. They walk long distances for water to drink and to bathe. Through the dusty crowded streets, two- and three-year-old barefoot children run naked and alone. What struck me most was not the poverty or the danger but the warmth of the people in the favelas. They made me feel at home and welcome. It made me reexamine the hood that I'd built my whole career rebuking. No matter how bad the projects may be in America, there's typically running water, electricity, food and a secure roof. That simple truth was life-changing.

October 21, 2012

Damn today is wifey's Birthday. I wish I was there to be with her, but I'm stuck in this shithole. I never realized how much these days meant to me until now. Someone I love so much and I can't see her, touch her, all because I fucked up. I know she feels the same way but love becomes somewhat of your enemy in here. I called her to wish her a Happy Birthday and to tell her that I love her but not being there hurts. Right now we would probably be in another country somewhere having a great time with each other, getting drunk like we were kids back in High School. This place makes me bitter and angry, that's why I say love becomes your enemy. 'Cause every time I think about the good times I should be sharing with my wife it breaks my heart to know that this freedom has been taken away from me. I try not to think about it, but it's all I think about. Sitting in this cell looking at the pics I have up of all of us and our beautiful family reminds me of all the good times we've shared over the years, the hard times too. But I honestly can't say bad times, our love has grown over the years and we're slowly but surely becoming best friends. We've been

together so long I couldn't see myself with any other woman. She
is my first, my last, my everything.

SOUL MATES!!!!
HAPPY BIRTHDAY BABY
JEFF HEARTS AISHA
LOL . . . XOXOXOXO

*

FOURTEEN

Sober

I WASN'T EXPECTING THAT SHIT IN A MILLION YEARS. THE WAY they arrested me was *bullshit*. I made a surprise appearance at a Lil Wayne show at the Beacon Theater in New York. I've known Lil Wayne since he was twelve years old. He and I collaborated on "Uh-Ohhh!!" for *The Mirror*. I had been laying low, so when he called me and asked me to come down to do a surprise performance with him, I was happy to do it. When he called me to the stage, the crowd went wild. I was feeling good about the show, happy that some people knew "The Mirror," and liked it.

After the show, I got into my Maybach, drove half a block and the cops pulled me over for speeding. First of all, you *can't* speed in a Maybach. It's a $400,000 car, which is half limo, half tank. It weighs about *nine trillion* pounds. It *ain't* made for racing. Secondly, they claimed it was a "routine stop"—except there were two undercovers, two undercover cars and six or seven officers there to make the arrest. Then they searched the car and found a gun in a side compartment.

Only four words would explain who they were: The Hip-Hop Task Force, the secret intelligence group that the NYPD formed in 2003. The *Village Voice* did a story on it. It's a group that was actually created for the sole purpose of keeping its eye on hip-hop artists and their entourages.

I wasn't even driving the damned car. My driver, Muhammad, RIP, was. I was in the back of the car, so the whole idea of a speeding violation for me doesn't even add up. Lil Wayne got arrested that same night on the same charge. He did *eight months* for that shit. Damned cops! They must have gotten mad medals for that shit, nabbing two rappers in one night.

The next morning after my arrest, I felt like an asshole. I have kids and I had gotten arrested, again. I tried to protect them as much as I could by never speaking about my legal problems in front of them. For a couple of years, I'd been buying time and doing everything I could to delay the inevitable. But, my time had come. I couldn't put it off anymore.

TAX EVASION WAS ANOTHER MISTAKE I made. Although the papers called it tax evasion, the official charge was Failure to File, which is a little different. I did pay taxes but just not enough. Where I come from, my Moms and grandparents were never fully educated on financial matters. The little bit of money my Moms ever had, she spent. And how could they educate me about something they didn't have?

My first experience with money came from hustling. We were all young and didn't know what to do with all that cash that was flowing in like water. When we got paid from drug sales, we just spent what we wanted and kept the rest in shoeboxes. It was not any real money. Drug money and hustle money is always temporary money. It flows right through your hands. Maybe a street hustler can pay some small bills and get some gold teeth, new sneakers, but only a few, at the very top, can get a new house or something that increases in value, as opposed to decreases in value.

When I started to really make money with music, for a while there, I still didn't know what to do with it. There were days that I would spend $100,000 in one day, knowing that I would make it again the next day at the next show. We spent all of our lives calling it "paper," which says something.

I'D BEEN BACK AND FORTH to court for years disputing the charges, paying fines and consulting with my lawyer about a plea bargain. There were *multiple* charges. I had been fighting hard to stay free but the time had come. I almost didn't have the heart to tell Moms that I was going to turn myself in but she needed to hear it from me. It was going to be all over the national news. I had put my family through so much already.

I was supposed to report to the jail in April, but I got two months to get my affairs in order. On June 8, 2011, I dragged myself and my family to report to prison. I dreaded the long drive into Manhattan. I dreaded the thought of leaving my family. There was not a dry eye in the car, as I drove us to the courthouse in Manhattan.

Always the joker, I said, "I'm going to turn myself in today but what we should really do is turn this car around and go to the airport and flee the country!"

No one laughed. They just smiled while tears rolled down everybody's faces, except for mine. I was finally being faced with the truth of who I was and what I had been doing.

THE JAIL SENTENCE STARTED with several brief stays at different facilities and then there was a formal sentencing where I would see my family again, in the courtroom.

My Moms and Ish were both crying at the federal sentencing proceedings. They were crying because they both knew what I knew, that I could get between thirty-six and sixty more months that would run *consecutively*. The moment of truth was upon us. As the proceedings started everything went silent for me. The court officer and the court reporter were moving in slow motion. Time had stopped. All I could hear were my own thoughts bumping up against each other inside my head. *I'm letting everyone down. My family. My friends. My fans.*

Stacey Richman, my lawyer, was up there doing the best she could for me. She was telling the judge of all of my accomplishments, including my travel to Kuwait for the USO tour to perform for the troops and being nominated for a Grammy Award.

The judge was unmoved.

I could faintly hear Stacey reciting a list of my charitable work, including nonviolence work that I did for local youth. The judge interrupted Stacey. "How ironic that the young man is an advocate for the very same thing that he is going to prison for." I had to say something on my own behalf, although that was not what Stacey and I had planned.

I almost felt like I had jinxed myself playing all those jail roles in movies like *Half Past Dead*, *Assault on Precinct 13*, and *Furnace*. The words "you reap what you sow" were running through my head.

The judge was speaking but I couldn't quite tune in to what she was saying.

Suddenly the words "high school graduation" popped into my head. I don't know if the judge said it or Ish whispered it into my ear from across the room, but my body suddenly went numb.

The judge said, "Mr. Atkins, are you okay?"

I must have stumbled forward. "Yes, your honor, I'm okay."

Finally, a tear rolled down my left cheek. I knew for sure with the thirty-six months pending, I would not be home for Brittney's high school graduation. My hurt turned to rage and I could feel my skin tightening and my heart racing inside my chest. I was angry with myself.

"Mr. Atkins, would you like to say anything on your own behalf?" the judge said, dutifully.

"Yes, your honor." Stacey furrowed her brow. I looked away.

"You may stand and speak, Mr. Atkins," the judge said.

When I was face-to-face with her, at that moment, I realized that whatever I said better be *good*. I was looking at possibly thirty-six months, which would destroy me. It could go either way.

I'm sure that the judge had heard plenty of sob stories from rich rappers trying to wiggle their way out of doing their full sentence. I was no different from them, but what I had to say to her was different to me because it was the first time I had ever begged.

I opened my mouth but nothing came out.

"Mr. Atkins, we are waiting," the judge said, impatiently.

I was shaken as I felt the impenetrable shell that had always protected me fall away from my body, freeing me to be humble.

"Your honor, the thought of missing my daughter's high school graduation is worse than any prison sentence you could give me."

"You've had all the chances that the law can possibly allow, Mr. Atkins. I see that from your rap sheet," she said, peering over her glasses. "You've been in the system since you were sixteen years old. *Nearly two decades.*"

"Your honor, my fate is in your hands and you don't know anything about me, except for what you see on that rap sheet. I'd like to tell you a little bit about who I really am."

"Mr. Atkins, we don't have all day."

"Your honor, I bet you didn't know that I've been with the same woman since junior high school. My wife's name is Aisha Atkins. She's here with me today. We have three incredible children, Brittney, Jeffrey Jr. and Jordan. My daughter is going to college in the fall after she graduates."

The judge finally looked up from her paper. "Go on."

"Your honor, I'm not the guy they portray me to be. I'm a good guy, a *family* man. Not a gangster. I'm just a normal guy who went through a bad time. I don't deserve to miss my daughter's high school graduation. I *can't* miss it."

"Mr. Atkins, what makes you different than anyone else who's in your position?"

"Your honor, I never graduated from high school. I dropped out in the eleventh grade. That has been a shame that I carry with me to this day. My Moms, who you see behind me, has never gotten to attend a high school graduation except for her own. I'm her only child. My sister was stillborn in 1982. I have disappointed my mother and my family too many times. I worked so hard for years so my own children could stay on the right track. I was crazy before but I now *understand* how important education is. It's the least I can do for my children."

"Go on," the judge said, her gaze softening.

"I'm a young man who's had a lot of success but unfortunately, I didn't always seek out the right people in my life. Your honor, I admit that I've been irresponsible and a poor role model, but I'm not a bad guy. You see that I have a family that loves me and supports me, even here. The media is trying to paint me as an evil rapper. I'm not that person anymore. You know what I do every day? Father my three children and be a husband to my wife. I never had a father of my own, your honor."

"Mr. Atkins, do you know how many performers I see with no fathers, children and wives? Have you said everything you needed to say?"

"No, your honor. I just want to say, we performers have an onstage persona and then we have who we really are, which is the side that no one ever sees. I've finally grown up over the last few years. I really want to break the cycle of undereducation, poverty and crime starting with myself . . . and my community. Like I said, my daughter will be attending college in the fall. That'll be the beginning. I *need* to see her graduate, your honor. My promise to Brittney eighteen years ago depends on it. Thank you for listening, your honor."

"What did you promise your daughter?"

"That I would raise her, guide her and *save* her."

THE JUDGE GAVE ME twenty-six months to run concurrently with my twenty months with the State, in prison, and two months of house arrest. I had already spent April and May at home on house arrest where I wore a monitor on my ankle that tracked my movement. I had parole officers coming in and out of my house unannounced to take urine samples from me once a week, making sure that I was clean. I felt like a fool. Aisha was charged with the task of keeping me in the house at all times and she would be asked to do it again at the end of my twenty months, when I returned.

Two years in jail would mean a dramatic loss of income for my family. I had bought houses for my mother and my grandmother. I'd sent Ish's sister Antoinette to college. I even remember the time after my first album that I took my boys on a shopping spree and the tab was $500,000. I had been frivolous with money for too long. This was yet another wake-up call. I realized that I needed to get rid of things and habits that I no longer needed. My mother would have to move out of her house and come and live with us. I had bought her a large four-bedroom house for her to live in alone. My mother's sister Dawn and brother, Dennis, both needed a place to stay, so I ended up taking care of all of them in that house. I didn't mind, but I was going to prison and we had to make some significant changes. I'd have to get rid of the Maybach and we'd all have to watch the money more carefully. I knew it would work out, just as it had when Brittney was born. We never missed a meal or a mortgage payment. What mattered most was that I'd be home to see my baby girl graduate.

WHILE MY JAIL SENTENCE was fast approaching, it was a dark and humbling period for me. It was the perfect time for me to make another creative album so I called in producer 7 Aurelius who had worked with me on *Pain Is Love*. I called the new album *PIL2, Pain Is Love 2*. Over the years I'd learned how the fame game worked. I understood that fans' love strictly depended on my hits, not my *music*. With *PIL2*, I'd see who was really listening because it was strictly for people who really loved music, not just hip-hop heads. *PIL2* didn't have party songs. It was an album with meaning, as I continued to grapple with the truth of myself.

On this album, I worked with a group of artists such as Leah Siegal and Anita Louise. I also brought in a Korean singer named Somong and vocalist Jon Doe. All of the tracks were musical and harmonic, with rapping but also a lot of melodies and vocals. Each song had meaningful lyrics that pertained to all of the questions in my head about where I'd been and where I was going.

On the album, I tried to paint pictures with sounds and lyrics. I felt these new sounds and sights were forcing my true fans to grow with me. To think differently, to be different themselves and to trust.

As I sat in the studio making *PIL2*, the candles burned in the darkness as I watched the film *Exit Through the Gift Shop* over and over again. It's a "documentary" by street artist Banksy, about an eccentric character played by the real-life street artist Mr. Brainwash. Mr. Brainwash becomes obsessed with street art. The character goes on a mission to find the aloof Banksy. Once he meets him and other street artists, he decides to become a street artist himself. The film looks at art, asking the question, What is art, actually? Who decides art's value, the artist or the audience? What makes it art: The materials used? The venue that displays it? Or simply popular opinion? What makes art authentic? Is there any such thing as inauthentic art?

As the movie played endlessly in the background of my late-night recording sessions, I got glimpses of it as I worked. The images of the artists and snatches of their dialogues dove into my subconscious. The actors were toying with the big questions that I was pondering, too. The more I watched the film, the harder I worked, tweaking each song as if it were my first. The songs were provocative and somewhat dark. There were titles like "Real Life Fantasy," "Drown," "Black Vodka" and "Strange Days." I worked and worked to make the album exciting and unusual. I wanted the album to be an original. I worked like a mad scientist, knowing this would be my last album for a while.

There was nothing to lose. I no longer had to care about beefs, fans, praise or disses. I was on my way out of the loop and on my way to my artistic self. It's what I had always wanted out of making music but didn't know it.

FIFTEEN

Changing

Lord, can we get a break
We ain't really happy here
When you look into our eyes
You see pain without fear

The inmates had been chanting that shit from my first album. I had written it for them to sing. It killed me that I was in prison with them, chanting my own prophetic words. *Black men singing for freedom.*

AT MY HOME in the New Jersey suburbs, "prison" had become a household word. Instead of Aisha feeling ashamed about me being in prison, several women consoled her with the news that their husbands had also gone to prison for white-collar crimes. The white-collar crimes seemed innocent, yet they still equaled time. Everyone in prison had breached the trust of people who had trusted them.

Aisha and the kids adjusted as well as they could, with a lot of tears that I never saw. Every weekend they would drive three hours to see me. I was usually tired on the visits because we were always up late the night before, watching movies, shooting the shit and acting like little kids sneaking around doing shit that we weren't supposed to. My man Smitty played lookout while we blew cigarette smoke into the vents so that the CO wouldn't find out. Q led the bread heists when we would hide bread in our stash box in the chow halls to help us add bread to our mostly meat shipments that we received in the mail. It was really high school shit, which is what we had been reduced to, kids in the playground.

Friday and Saturday nights, we were allowed to stay up until two a.m., looking at each other in disbelief at the bare, smelly rec room's pale cinderblock walls. In the beginning, we all looked forward to the late nights, but after a while, it became a drag. I started leaving the fellas in the rec room and going to bed. We were all devastated at the shittyness of life. To pass time, we would escape with entertainment. We would watch movies that would take us far away from that place.

Fresh haircut, fresh greens and a pair of the new sneakers that Aisha sent me were what I would put on to go down to meet my family in the visitation room, otherwise known as the dance floor. I was glad that a glass divider didn't come between us. As I walked out to see them every week, I would do my best to appear okay. I was dealing with this shit the best I could.

They came every week with rare exceptions. I spoke to the kids almost every day. We tried to keep it as normal as we could. I hoped for them that it just felt like I was away on tour. But I wasn't. Instead of hitting stadiums and stages, I was touring the bowels of America's broken correctional system.

I did not go directly to prison. Like the animal that I was treated like, I was regularly shuttled from prison to prison, bus ride after bus ride; pushed, shoved, insulted and neglected.

My first stop was Rikers for three days. Then I was taken to Ulster Correctional Facility. It was the place they take you before they place you somewhere permanent. Oneida was next. It was eventually shut down due to budget cuts. From there I went to Essex County for almost a month, waiting to be sentenced for tax stuff. While I was being shuttled from Oneida to Essex County, the marshals went right past the exit for my house, the place that Aisha was taking the kids to school, making their meals and paying our bills. I couldn't stand to think about what I was missing.

From the Green Monster I was shipped back to Oneida for a few days before it was closed down. The marshals were cool. They took good care of me while I was in their custody. A few days later I was moved to Mid-State Correctional Facility, where I stayed for the duration of my incarceration. The next stop was Metropolitan Detention Center in Brooklyn, which is a holding facility before a federal sentence is decided on, then to Ray Brook in upstate New York, an hour from Canada. By the time I reached Ray Brook, with only a few months to go, I told Aisha not to come visit me anymore, I was sick of the whole fucking thing. We all knew I'd be home *soon*.

With all of that moving around, every time I went to a new prison, it felt like the first day of high school. Everyone inside has their guard up. I learned early on if you are solid and confident and don't take shit from anyone, no one fucks with you. Once I got cool with everybody, they opened up to me and told me that they were fans of mine. Some of them told me that they thought I would be stuck-up but once they realized that I was a cool dude, it was all good and they could really talk to me.

I KNEW THAT AISHA took her time getting dressed to visit me, not wanting to violate the strict dress code for women. After long drives spent with a car full of somber passengers, she would never risk being turned away. Aisha had seen women being turned away at the security gate, simply for their inappropriate clothes. Visiting women were not permitted to be stylish or provocative. Ish usually wore the same sort of thing every week. Flat leather boots, UGGs or sneakers. She was to wear "clothes that didn't accentuate." It didn't matter to me what she was wearing, whatever she wore warmed my heart as if it was the first time I saw her in shop class in the eighth grade.

The four-hour visits were pleasant and as unemotional as we could make them. Aisha was mostly all cried out and I didn't cry at all. I had been too busy looking at my life, regretting my choices and understanding why I was there and why I'd never, ever be there again. Our visits reminded me of back in the day when we had been giddy and excited to tell each other entertaining stories that would make us both laugh out loud.

In the visitation room, Ish would hold my hand as she talked about Brittney and her newest teenage dramas. I would then tell her about what was going on with me, which was always much of the same. Aisha and I, as always, could talk about everything under the sun, but we were careful not to get too deep. Everything was already too heavy for us. The laughter was gone.

When the weather was warm, Jeffrey, Jordan and I would often hit the yard and play a couple of games of chess and checkers. I just listened mostly to my boys as they each told me of their elementary and high school adventures. We would talk about sports, and sometimes I would give them some life lessons, especially when Jeff Jr. would ask me questions about prison. I'd always say the same thing,

"You see where I am? This is the place that you *never* want to be. Some people romanticize prison, making it seem like some sort of badge of honor. Prison is not to be proud of. I'm ashamed of it. I should've never been here."

It was painful to watch them grow from a distance. It was painful to see that they could still grow without me. It felt tragic that I wouldn't be at next week's big football game or able to help Jordan with his book report. I kept smiling and hugging and telling them how much I loved them. I was *missing* so much.

I loved my boys for being with Aisha and helping her through this. The one who didn't visit often was Brittney. There were reasons. She had acting classes on Saturdays and I didn't want her to miss them. I didn't want the kids to miss anything that they had to do to visit me in prison. I also understood that she didn't want to see me like that. Brittney didn't want to be participate in anything that would take two more years out of her life with me.

The fact that we were not separated by a glass wall made the visits even harder. The feel of Ish's warm hand in mine, the feel of her lips when she kissed me goodbye, was tough. Saying goodbye was the worst part of the visit. I never wanted to let them go.

MY OLDEST CHILD, Brittney, is a beautiful, talented young woman who is determined to have her own successes, without my help. I look at her and I see that she's just like me. She has a lot of energy and she wants to be an actor and she will. Brittney and I have a strange and strong relationship. Brittney has endured the majority of my absences throughout her young life because of my career. For her, there have been too many disappointments. Her frustration at my absences can only pale in comparison to my own fury at failing her.

AT THIRTEEN YEARS OLD, my son Jeffrey reminds me of me. He thinks it's cool that Ja Rule is his dad. He's real laid-back and cool most of the time, but his fatal flaw is that he has an explosive temper, just like me. He watches my every move, so I am forced to be a better man. The only way that I can truly be a role model for him is to be the man I want him to become.

I tell my boys: "Don't make the mistakes I've made." "I went through what I have so you don't have to." "I had to learn everything the hard way so you don't have to." I sound like a broken record sometimes, but I'm just making sure that they know how much I care. They are young Black men in America and there's a lot that they need to know. I try to shield them from too many tough conversations, but life continues to bring us the big questions and even tougher answers.

My kids have always gone to school with kids of all cultures. It's more important to me that they become comfortable with all kinds of people because that's the world we live in. Aisha and I share Black history and a Black perspective with our children, as much as we can. The irony of Black success is that no matter how far we climb, we're always reminded of who we are in the eyes of others. I teach them those kinds of lessons, too.

My youngest son, Jordan, is ten, and he's too young to understand most of what has happened to me. Jordan reminds me of myself when I was young. He's never afraid to dance or sing in front of strangers, which is exactly how I was as a kid. That boy is totally animated and creative.

The one thing prison did do for me was to give me some time to rest and reflect on my life. I thought about the many mistakes that I made. Prior to being incarcerated, I was spiraling out of control. I was riding around with a gun. What if I had to use that gun? The twenty months could easily have been twenty years.

I needed this time to think, too. It allowed me the chance to think about how I was living. When I started out in music, I thought I could take everybody with me. But that wasn't the case. Some people are not ready for this journey because the vision is not theirs. I learned that some people can see only what is in front of them, while others have large dreams and a determination to get there. I used to run with twenty, thirty people. I couldn't control them all. This was particularly troubling because what they did would reflect upon me and my image. If someone in my crew did something bad, all the news will report is Ja Rule's entourage did this and that. I'm the one who pays the price for their poor decisions, as well as my own. I had to learn this the hard way.

Prison also gave me the time to learn who I am. I recognized that I have to control my circle and those in it. I realized who my real friends were because they were the ones to visit me in jail. I saw who hung around during the upside and walked away during the downswing. Now people can come, but not necessarily sit at my table.

OTHER THAN VISITOR DAYS, prison days were long and hopeless. Prison was like *Groundhog Day*. Everything was painfully the same. The days stretched out before us like a blank sheet of paper and each of us had to decide how we were going to fill it, but a lot of us didn't know where to start. I had a job. They had me doing lawns and grounds in the morning and porter work in the afternoon. It wasn't bad, it got me out of that filthy cell. It got me outside.

During rec time, I hit the weights. I gained about thirty pounds. People thought I was lifting Toyotas in that bitch. Seriously, working out allowed me to free my mind from everything that was constantly swirling around in my head. It's the only way to do your time. In prison you have to think *inside* the box because you don't want to get yourself reminiscing of things that are outside the box because it hurts too deeply.

Those of us who didn't have jobs would stay as idle inside as they had been outside. Some guys were sleeping late, getting into mischief, fighting with one another or trying to mentally prepare for the day they would be released.

My first few nights in prison, I would have the craziest dreams. I felt like I was seeing demons. It was as if the devil would come into my cell and hold me down. I was seeing evil every night. I would wake up to COs with their flashlights in my face. All I could see of them were shadows. It would take hours for me to fall back to sleep. I would stay up staring out the window and then start writing.

I was so grateful that Aisha was able to send me boxes of food, so I didn't have to eat the chow. Since I was working out and getting healthier than I had ever been in my life, I wanted to eat good food. I was only able to receive thirty-five pounds per month and Aisha would carefully measure and weigh the boxes, sending twenty pounds at the beginning of the month and fifteen towards the end. She would send me sliced fresh meats for sandwiches, green vegetables, organic oatmeal for breakfast and fresh fruits. My ride or die always comes through for me.

One critical memory was that there was a crisis with my oldest son, Jeffrey, while I was away. L'il Rule had a friend from school. He was invited to sleep over at their house with some other boys about a year ago. A few days after the sleepover, the child's father called Aisha saying that his Rolex watch was missing from the house. As much as he told Aisha that he *didn't* think that Jeffrey had taken it, *we* understood why he was calling. . . . *Of course,* blame it on the Black kid. Even if his father is Ja Rule. Even if Jeffrey has always had his own gold and diamond jewelry. . . . It just boils down to the fact that Jeffrey was the *Black kid* at the sleepover, so he was the most likely candidate to have lifted the watch. Aisha was *enraged.*

Where was Jeffrey's father when that shit went down? Away in prison, fitting the stereotype, further burying my innocent son in four hundred years of our painful history that never seems to end. The pain of my son even having to deal with that man's suspicion is still more than I can bear. After yelling into the phone with Ish, I punched the four cement walls that held me. My skin crawled with the rage that I wasn't there to set that man straight; man to man, father to father. I wasn't there for that man to see in my eyes that I've been through *too much* to raise a thief. But I wasn't there to defend my son's honor, which pains me to this day.

EVER SINCE ELEMENTARY SCHOOL, PS 186, I have been interacting with a variety of races. I have the ability to fit in wherever I am. I could play with white kids and Black kids with no problem. Nothing has changed.

Part of my prison sentence was spent in state facilities where I met Alan Hevesi and Dennis Kozlowski. When I was sent to federal prison, they wanted to put me in solitary confinement for my own protection. But I didn't want to live alone in a dark closet. I wanted to be in general population with other guys like me. It was a breath of fresh air. I was happy to be around a larger group after being at Mid-State.

In state prison I spent my time in protective custody with older white millionaires and tycoons.

They stay in *their* circles and keep us in ours. You best believe, when they come into our circle, there's money to be made, but most of it for them. It's kind of funny that I would meet these guys in prison. Alan Hevesi was the former New York State Comptroller, who admitted to taking $1 million for his own personal use. Then there was Dennis Kozlowski (I called him "Koz"), the former CEO of Tyco Corporation, an industrial conglomerate (now broken up) that was referred to as "Little GE." He allegedly took tens of millions from his employer to support a lavish lifestyle. Larry Salander, owner of Salander-O'Reilly Galleries, allegedly stole millions from artists and art collectors such as actor Robert De Niro and professional tennis player John McEnroe, whom he had been a personal friend with for years. All of these rich muthafuckas allegedly *stole* millions of dollars. I realized they were just like me. We'd all gotten caught up in the sticky web of temptation.

I learned a lot from those guys, but the most important thing I learned is that the predator of temptation is color-blind. Although the system may treat white inmates better than Black inmates or celebrities better than the "general population," when you look into the eyes of guys from both sides, they all have the same look of shame, sorrow and regret. If all of us could have just turned back the clock one minute or one hour before we made that wrong decision, we wouldn't have been there.

We were inside when Obama's reelection campaign was in full force. Alan Hevesi and me kicked it a lot about politics. He was a Democrat, like me, so we had a lot in common in this area. Hevesi was also a Knicks fan so, whenever we could, we'd watch the games together. We were all just regular dudes doing time.

Dennis Kozlowski kept to himself a lot. He acted as though he was above everyone else. I don't want to judge him because everyone deals with disgrace differently. "Koz's" job in prison was being a laundry porter. He stayed to himself a lot in the laundry room. Ironically, he was the worst laundry porter I had ever seen. He always brought our shit all balled up in a bag. We referred to his room as his office and we all would bust out laughing at the irony.

Larry Salander, the art dealer, was another great dude. He shared a lot with me about art, and the way value is determined. He believed that the classic paintings by Monet or Renoir should value much higher than a Warhol or Basquiat. It was not that way in the marketplace, and it drove him crazy. Speaking to him reminded me of the Banksy film, regarding how we quantify art and its value. He was passionate about it and he reminded me of myself. He had created a once very well respected, internationally known art business based on passion and the compulsion to change the art world, whether it needed changing or not.

But these white boys don't mean nothing to me, and I don't mean nothing to them.

Dominick was a seventeen-year-old guy who was important to me. He was doing one a half to three for getting in a harmless fight at school. The thing is, Dominick, a Black kid, went to a white school and the white parents pressed criminal charges against Dominick. Even though Dominick's parents are hardworking, middle-class people, it didn't protect their son from the realities of life.

I took Dominick under my wing. We played basketball and talked a lot as I shared my life's experiences. I also looked out for him as I would my own son, even though Dominick has a father. Talking to Dominick made me think of my own kids. I'm always willing to help, because in our community, our kids are us and we are them.

ON MAY 7, 2013, I was released from federal prison, and everything is back to normal, as if I never left. I'm still touring the world for shows, only this time my wife is right by my side. I'm back on the sidelines of football games and wrestling matches with Jeff and Jordan. And I'm happy to say I was able to see Brittney graduate, and even prouder to say she's now in college at Hampton University. I don't think my kids are going to be anyone's job security.

I'm currently working on my new album, *Genius Loves Company*, my new reality show called *Follow the Rules*, as well as producing and starring in several upcoming movies. And somewhere in the midst of all of that, I managed to add "author" to my list of accomplishments by bringing you my life story, my memoir, *Unruly*.

ACKNOWLEDGMENTS

There are many people who have helped to make this book a reality, too many to name them all. First, I would like to thank God, who makes everything possible. I want to thank my family: you all mean the world to me and I appreciate your contributions to *Unruly*. Thanks to Carol Mann, my literary agent. You were right, Tracy Sherrod would be a devoted, caring editor. Kim Green, it has been nice working with you, but next time I'm going to buy you a tape recorder! I sincerely appreciate my Flavor Unit family. Thanks to Queen Latifah and Shakim. A special thanks to my manager, Ron Robinson, for clearing the permissions (not!). My HarperCollins family has been incredible in many ways: Thanks to Jonathan Burnham, Kathy Schneider, Leah Wasielewski, Katie O'Callaghan, Leslie Cohen, Kathleen Baumer, Robin Bilardello and Richard Ljoenes. Thanks to Kyran Cassidy for the legal read: "I did not have sexual relations with that woman!" Thanks to Muhammad Ali, Tupac Shakur, Steve Harvey, Michael Jordan, Martin Luther King Jr., John F. Kennedy Jr., Malcolm X, Mao, and Mandela—your example and discussions about manhood have been invaluable and have influenced me in many ways.

ABOUT THE AUTHOR

—

JEFFREY ATKINS, more popularly known by his stage name Ja Rule, is a rapper, singer, songwriter and actor from Queens, New York. He has released seven studio albums since 1999 and has sold over thirty million records worldwide. In addition to having Grammy and American Music Award nominations, he has won several awards, including MTV Music Awards, World Music Awards, Teen Choice Awards, NAACP Image Awards, and *GQ*'s Man of the Year Award. He lives in New Jersey with his wife and children.